The Goal of Life and How to Attain It

SPIRITUAL SADHANAS FOR EVERYONE

J.P. VASWANI

GITA PUBLISHING HOUSE
PUNE, (INDIA).
www.dadavaswanisbooks.org

Published by:
Gita Publishing House
Sadhu Vaswani Mission,
10, Sadhu Vaswani Path,
Pune -411 001, (India).
gph@sadhuvaswani.org

Second Edition

ISBN: 978-93-80743-42-4

Printed by:
Mehta Offset Pvt. Ltd.
Mehta House,
A-16, Naraina Industrial Area II,
New Delhi-110 028, (India).
info@mehtaoffset.com

Other Books and Booklets by Dada J.P. Vaswani

In English:
10 Commandments of A Successful Marriage
108 Pearls of Practical Wisdom
108 Simple Prayers of A Simple Man
108 Thoughts on Success
114 Thoughts on Love
A Little Book of Life
A Simple And Easy Way To God
A Treasure of Quotes
Around The Camp Fire
Begin The Day With God
Bhagavad Gita in a Nutshell
Burn Anger Before Anger Burns You
Daily Inspiration
Daily Inspiration (Booklet)
Destination Happiness
Dewdrops of Love
Does God Have Favourites?
Ecstasy and Experiences
Formula For Prosperity
Gateways to Heaven
God In Quest of Man
Good Parenting
Gurukul
Gurukul II
How To Overcome Depression
I am a Sindhi
In 2012 All Will Be Well
Joy Peace Pills
Kill Fear Before Fear Kills You
Ladder of Abhyasa
Lessons Life Has Taught Me
Life After Death
Management Moment by Moment
Mantras For Peace Of Mind
Many Paths: One Goal
Nearer, My God, To Thee!
New Education Can Make the World New
Peace or Perish
Positive Power of Thanksgiving
Questions Answered
Sadhu Vaswani : His Life And Teachings
Saints For You and Me
Saints With A Difference
Secrets of Health And Happiness
Shake Hand With Life
Short Sketches of Saints Known & Unknown
Sketches of Saints Known & Unknown
Stop Complaining: Start Thanking!
Swallow Irritation Before Irritation Swallows You
Teachers are Sculptors
The Little Book of Freedom From Stress
The Little Book of Prayer
The Little Book of Service
The Little Book of Success
The Little Book of Wisdom
The Little Book of Yoga
The Magic of Forgiveness
The Perfect Relationship: Guru and Disciple
The Seven Commandments of the Bhagavad Gita
The Terror Within
The Way of Abhyasa (How To Meditate)
Thus Have I Been Taught
Tips For Teenagers
What You Would Like To know About Karma
What You Would Like To know About Hinduism

What To Do When Difficulties Strike
Why Do Good People Suffer?
You Are Not Alone God Is With You!

Story Books:
101 Stories For You And Me
25 Stories For Children and also for Teens
It's All A Matter of Attitude
Snacks For The Soul
More Snacks For The Soul
Break The Habit
The Lord Provides
The Heart of a Mother
The King of Kings
The One Thing Needful
The Patience of Purna
The Power of Good Deeds
The Power of Thought
Trust Me All in All or Not at All
Whom Do You Love the Most
You Can Make A Difference

In Hindi:
Aalwar Santon Ki Mahan Gaathaayen
Atmik Jalpaan
Aapkay Karm, Aapkaa Bhaagy Banaatay Hein
Atmik Poshan
Bhakton Ki Uljhanon Kaa Saral Upaai
Bhale Logon Ke Saath Bura Kyon?
Dainik Prerna
Dar Se Mukti Paayen
Ishwar Tujhe Pranam
Jiski Jholi Mein Hain Pyaar
Krodh Ko Jalayen Swayam Ko Nahin
Laghu Kathayein
Mrutyu Hai Dwar... Phir Kya?
Nava Pushp (Bhajans In Hindi and Sindhi)
Prarthna ki Shakti
Pyar Ka Masiha
Sadhu Vaswani: Unkaa Jeevan Aur Shikshaayen
Safal Vivah Ke Dus Rahasya
Santon Ki Leela
Sri Bhagavad Gita: Gaagar Mein Saagar

In Marathi:
Krodhala Shaanth Kara, Krodhane Ghala Ghalnya Purvee (Burn Anger Before Anger Burns You)
Jiski Jholi Mein Hain Pyaar
Life After Death
Pilgrim of Love
Sind and the Sindhis
Sufi Sant (Sufi Saints of East and West)
What You Would Like To Know About Karma

Other Publications:

Recipe Books:
90 Vegetarian Sindhi Recipes
Di-li-cious Vegetarian Recipes
Simply Vegetarian

Books on Dada J. P. Vaswani:
A Pilgrim of Love
Dada J.P. Vaswani: His Life and Teachings
Dada J.P. Vaswani's Historic Visit to Sind
Dost Thou Keep Memory
How To Embrace Pain
Living Legend
Moments with a Master

CONTENTS

Foreword

Manush janam durlabh hai mile na barambar,
joon drakht se phal pak bhoon gire, lage na phir dar...

— Sant Kabir

As always, Kabir has the gift of expressing the most profound truths in the simplest and most effective words: this human life is indeed rare and precious: it will not come to us again and again. Just as the ripe fruit which falls from the tree can never be attached to the tree again, so too, this life, if wasted away, can never be regained.

Why is the human birth so precious? The answer is simple. It is only through the human birth that we can attain liberation. It is only through the human birth that we can rid ourselves of the burden of *karma* and break from the bonds of life, death and rebirth. That is why it is said that even in the heavenly world, the denizens yearn for the human birth. The purpose of the human birth is to work towards a higher life, the life beautiful. But sadly, many of us fritter away this life in worthless pursuits, little realising the value of that which we throw away so carelessly.

It is strange, but we look for value addition in everything we do. We question the worth and the price we pay for everything, including medical treatment and education. A man who undergoes knee replacement surgery asks his surgeon, "For how many years will this knee be good for me?" A student who joins the MBA programme demands to know whether it will fetch her a job that will recover her fees in two months. "What am I going to get out of this?" is a constant refrain in business, investment and trade.

Are you asking yourself the same kind of questions about your life? Are you living your precious human life meaningfully, consciously, purposefully?

I know that the answer to that question is not easy! But you will agree with me that we need to think about it, at least occasionally.

True, we all love life! We want to make the most of it. We long for happiness, peace and fulfillment in all that we do. But do we know the purpose of this life, the goal of this life?

The meaning of life has been one of the fundamental issues in philosophy, theology and religion. Since the dawn of civilisation, men of thought have grappled with such questions as: Who am I? Where do I come from? Whither am I going? What is the purpose for which I was born? How may I fulfill that purpose?

When you begin to ask these questions of yourself, you begin to realise that there is much more to life than seeking pleasure, worldly success, material wealth or even happiness. Somehow, all these 'desires' are short-lived as far as fulfillment is concerned. There must be more to life than this, you feel.

I do not believe I am exaggerating when I say: in this materialistic age in which we live, several people have come to realise that the meaning and significance of life is not to be found in amassing wealth or finding the life partner of your dreams. This is why more and more people are turning to spirituality, especially the practices and ideas of the Eastern religions, to seek answers to these questions.

Hinduism outlines four *purusharthas* or goals of life: *artha, kama, dharma and moksha* – or, to settle for a simple translation, wealth, desire, duty and liberation. And the best part of these goals is that you do not have to choose any one: you can legitimately choose and pursue all four, as you evolve spiritually. It may also happen that as you achieve each goal, your consciousness may rise until you decide that ultimately, there is only one goal that matters.

As for me, I believe that the purpose of this life is to grow in purity and perfection. Perfection is not to be dismissed as an impossible dream! Like excellence, the pursuit of perfection is itself a worthy goal. This pursuit is made possible by the fact that God, who is the essence of all perfection, dwells within each one of us. When we become aware of this fact at the conscious level, half the journey is completed.

According to the Sufis, every spiritual aspirant has to take three journeys:

1. The first journey is a journey of wandering. We live, we move about, we act and react; but we are unaware of what we are and where we are heading. During the first journey man wanders endlessly and moves away from Truth. The restless mind pushes man to seek all the pleasures of the world and he gets caught in worldly affairs, forgetting the purpose of his journey. We may easily recognise that this is the journey that most of us are currently pursuing! We are so wrapped up in worldly pursuits that we are quite, quite unconscious of any goal that is beyond material concerns.

Some years ago, I was invited to Nashik, a city situated about 210 kms. to the north-west of Pune. The distance is usually covered in about four hours by road, but on our outward journey, the traffic was so heavy and there were delays due to ongoing work on the highway, that we took over five hours to reach the city. My friend who took me in his car said that the delay was needless and could have been avoided, as he believed there was a short cut which if followed could have saved us about an hour.

When we left for Pune the same evening, it was the same friend who took the wheel of the car. "Dada, they kept you on the road far too long in the morning," he said to me with great feeling. "Just watch, I'm going to take you back through the short cut I know. Believe me, we will be back in Pune in about three hours!"

We drove at a good speed, having left the congested Pune-Nashik highway and taken a detour. The road was definitely clear and comparatively free of traffic; but I noticed that there were practically no signposts, and definitely none indicating the way to Pune or any of the towns near to Pune. After we had driven for about half an hour, I said to my friend, "May be we should stop at the next village or tea-stall and enquire whether we are on the right road."

"But there is no need for that Dada," he assured me. "See, we have already travelled 70 km. from Nashik; in just under two hours we will be in Pune!"

We drove on, and now, the road had become narrow and difficult to navigate. It was winter and darkness fell soon. I noticed that not only were there no signs to Pune, but that we were not even passing through known, familiar places en route. In the darkness, I saw a motor cyclist driving towards us, and I insisted that the car be stopped, much to the annoyance of my friend. We hailed the motor cyclist, who stopped politely to answer our queries; the truth was that since we stopped right in the middle of the narrow road, he could not get past us!

I greeted him and asked him, "Sir, how far is it to Pune from this place?"

"Pune?" he asked, puzzled. "Pune? But what are you doing on this road if you are headed for Pune?" And now, he was so genuinely concerned that he said, "Wait, let me explain." He parked his motor bike carefully off the road, and came back to my open window. "Sir, you are way out of your route! You are actually heading towards Shirdi! And there is no junction ahead where you can turn and head towards Pune. Sir, not only have you taken the wrong road, you have travelled too far to head back to Pune on this road! Now, I am sorry to say you have to head back all the way you travelled on this road, and hit the main Nashik-Pune highway!"

"Thank you, brother," I said to him, and turning to my friend at the wheel, I said politely, "You heard the man; now we must turn back and retrace our path to the Pune highway."

Though he was quite crestfallen by now, my friend was not ready to accept his mistake. "Maybe we have gone slightly off route," he said, "but surely, there's no need to go back all the way! I suggest we drive a little farther, and we are sure to take a right turn that will lead us to Pune!"

"I don't think so," I replied gently. "We can't keep moving ahead just because we have travelled this far on the wrong route. It is far better to make a U-Turn and head back to where we left the highway."

You are sure to have guessed the significance of the incident I have narrated. We set off on our worldly journey, convinced that it is the best route, adamant about our own goals, unheeding of all warning signs that tell us we are not on the right track. But a point comes in our life when we have to make that critical U-Turn back to God! For some of us, this realisation comes from within; for others, it is an awakening facilitated by the Guru. In either case, it is an important stage in our life, when we decide that the road that we are following is actually taking us farther and farther away from God, and that it is time to acknowledge our error, give up our misguided, misdirected wandering, and take that U-Turn to God!

2. The second journey begins with this U-Turn that follows the awakening of the soul. It begins with the realisation that we have lost precious time, and that we have to return home – to God. For long have we floundered. For long have we wandered. It is time to go back. A voice within us urges, "Awake. Awake. Return to your original home." The road we have taken has taken us far from

our goal. Now, we realise, it is time to retrace our steps, repair the damage done, and make up for all the precious time we have lost. When this awareness hits us – I use the word *hit* deliberately, because it is a sharp and painful awakening – we are disturbed and unsettled, even slightly disoriented. We begin to question the worth and value of all that we have achieved in worldly terms. We are seized by a sudden feeling of restlessness, a feeling of discontent which in turn leads to self-interrogation, introspection and a review and re-evaluation of our chosen goals and objects. "There must be more to life than this!" is the one thought that impels us at this stage. And now begins the second journey – the journey back to God!

Thus, we set out in the right direction, at long last. Now begins the serious, persistent search for God. This is the quest that has taken *yogis, rishis, munis* and *jignasus* to river banks, to *tapobanas*, to mountain tops, to temples and shrines. Realised souls find Him whom they seek, without too much trouble. But the rest of us are not so fortunate. We wander hither and thither; many places beckon us and we are lost in these wanderings. But let me assure you, if we are set on our goal, we find God sooner or later. For I truly believe, He helps us all the way. For every two steps we take towards Him, He comes closer to us with sure and swift steps. If the wanderings of the first journey took us away from God, the second journey takes us slowly, surely towards Him whom we seek! It is a journey Godward!

3. The third journey starts when we have attained our destination. It is the beautiful journey *in* God. Not away from Him, not towards Him, but *in* Him! It is the journey of the final blissful Union. It is the journey which will help us realise that He whom we sought is not really a destination apart from us, but that we are actually a part of Him! It takes us to a final point of no regret, no return and no more wandering; for our quest is at an end. We lose ourselves in God so that we may never, ever lose our way again! We lose our narrow, individual identity, to find our true self in

God. *Na ham! Na ham! Tu ho! Tu ho!* This is Oneness with God. This is the ultimate Bliss, this is *sat-chit-ananda!*

Let me explain what this Oneness is all about. It is self-annihilation to achieve self-realisation. In the words of a poet, "it is the desire of the moth for the star". Here is a little parable to help you understand this Oneness that I speak of.

One day, a seeker on the path knocked at the door of a Guru. A voice from inside the room asked, "Who are you?" The devotee replied, "Master, it is me." The voice from inside said, "There cannot be two beings here, you and Me. Here, there is only one being, the Supreme Being. You may please go back."

After several years, the devotee returned and knocked on the door. The voice from inside asked, "Who are you?" He replied, "My Beloved, there is only One and that is You." At once the door opened, the Guru himself came out and embraced the seeker. The Guru said, "We are one. There is neither you nor I. We have always been one." This is the Principle of Oneness.

As we are the children of God, we are a part of Him, we are a speck, a ray of the Supreme Being. How can we be separate from Him? There is ONENESS all around us, we have to realise and experience this Oneness. And this is where the third and final journey takes us.

The first journey may be the result of an unheeding, unaware attitude; the second journey begins with the dawn of true awareness; and the third and final journey is the journey towards utter self-annihilation (and, paradoxically) to ultimate Self-Realisation! The Realisation that God and I are One!

Psychologists tell us that there are three 'states' in which human beings exist: the waking state (*jagrut*), the sleeping state (*sushupti*) and the dreaming state (*swapna*).

Perhaps psychology stops a little short; for our ancient sages spoke of a fourth state which they called *turiya*– a state of which most of us are unaware.

An American friend once said to me, "Here in the Western World, we have three states of awareness which are different from yours: we are asleep, we are awake, or we are watching TV!"

Perhaps Westerners are not the only ones; many of us live in complete ignorance of this whole dimension of awareness that exists within us.

The question is, how many of us are willing to explore this kingdom within?

We are content to live our lives on the surface. Superficiality characterises everything we do. We judge other people by the clothes they wear and the cars they drive. We occupy our minds with what we would like to eat, what we would like to buy and what we could do to impress friends and neighbours. At the farthest, we save for the future and we make sure that there is enough money for us to spend in old age.

In our constant state of superficial existence, we continue to ignore the world within. In our persistent chase after shadow-shapes and worldly wealth, we lose sight of our inner consciousness. We emphasise speech, action and outward show; we forget that there is a far more valuable aspect to life called reflection, contemplation, introspection. Men and women of speech and action, there are very many; alas, men and women of reflection and contemplation, there are very few.

A leading practitioner of meditation in the U.S. once pointed out that several cultures and religions simply do not teach people to focus on the world within them; their emphasis is often on words, rites and rituals; on a form or a Being or Spirit *outside;* thus the innermost spirit remains out of reach of most people.

The Indian tradition on the other hand, has always placed great value on meditation, reflection and contemplation – on the state of inner silence and inner stillness. For it is in this state that we will find tranquility, serenity, self-knowledge and true awareness. In this state, too, we will experience true freedom – freedom from fear, desire, tension, insecurity and complexes that haunt us in the waking state. In this state of inner consciousness, we will also discover our own Divinity – that we are not the bodies we wear, we are not the insignificant, pathetic, frail creatures that we take ourselves to be; we will discover that we are the immortal *atman*, the eternal, infinite spirit that is *Sat-chit-ananda* – pure, true, eternal Bliss!

It is my firm belief that this bliss is the birthright of every human being who has been blessed with the gift of life. You may be a youngster, preparing yourself to meet the challenges of the adult world; you may be a householder, to whom the care of a spouse and family is entrusted; you may be a professional trapped willy nilly in the rat race of competition and progress; you may be any of these or all of these and a seeker who has felt the thirst for truth.

I claim kinship with each and everyone of you – as a fellow human being, a brother in the family of God's creation, and as a fellow pilgrim on the journey of life. In the following pages I wish to share with you some of the simple *sadhanas* that I have learnt at the feet of my Gurudev Sadhu Vaswani and other Great Ones, that can make your life meaningful and worthwhile, as you decide to make that crucial U-Turn towards God.

– J. P. Vaswani

What is *Sadhana?*

In its basic form, the Sanskrit word *sadhana* is "the means of accomplishing something". To be more specific, it refers to a spiritual practice prescribed by ancient Indian religions, specially Hinduism and Buddhism. In short, *sadhana* is a spiritual discipline which is essential for all seekers of truth. But, as we may appreciate, every seeker after truth is different in temperament, in personality, in mental and spiritual strength. Therefore, there are several *sadhanas* or techniques available to the seeker on the path to self-realisation, perfection or liberation.

There are literally hundreds of *sadhanas* or means that one can undertake in pursuit of spiritual growth: we can take to prayer, which is one of the simplest and easiest; we can take to *puja* or organised ritual worship; we can choose meditation, which is nothing but a journey inward in pursuit of truth; we can choose *japa yoga*, which is intensely focused chanting of a sacred *mantra;* there are tougher austerities too, like fasting, penance, *tapasya* and so on.

Gurudev Sadhu Vaswani who has been the inspiration, the guide, the guardian and the leading light of my life, offered us a simple, straightforward *sadhana* which each and everyone could practise effortlessly: the three S- *sadhana* of Silence, *Sangha* and Service. He urged us to practise silence everyday; he emphasised the spiritual fellowship that was available to us at the *satsang;* and, above all, he urged that our life, our wealth, our talent and our time were all but a loan given to us by the Almighty, to be poured out in selfless service to those less fortunate than ourselves.

Spend a little time in silent communion with God, everyday. Attend the *satsang* regularly. And do whatever you can to alleviate the sufferings of others, to make others happy!

Silence, *sangha* (fellowship) and service! If only we could follow these simple techniques of *sadhana* we would indeed find our lives transformed!

Why should we practise *sadhana?* What will it achieve for us? What will we get out of it? These are questions that many people ask themselves when they hear about *sadhana,* and its necessity for the seeker.

If these questions arise in your mind too, I can offer you a simple answer: there is a simple input-output ratio that operates in *sadhana;* you will get as much out of it as you put into it. Put in sincerity, dedication, commitment, faith and perseverance: and you will achieve your goal – indeed, you will achieve much more than you expect, with the grace of God.

At this point, you may come up with yet another question: if the grace of God is all that it is described to be, why should we fritter away our effort in *sadhanas?* Isn't it better to leave our Liberation in His safe hands, and just live our daily life? Moreover, our saints and sages tell us that spiritual progress can only happen with the grace of God. Isn't it better for that Divine grace to drop from heaven on us like the gentle rain?

To this question too, I have a simple answer: why wait for God's grace when you are not sure whether you have deserved it by your actions in this birth and in all the countless births that have gone before this one? His grace is sure to come to you when you work for it sincerely; *God helps those who help themselves* is not just a commonplace statement; it is the proven truth. The great saints and sages of this land undertook the greatest austerities and penances to attain Liberation. How then can we show reluctance to undertake a few disciplines for such a great goal?

Liberation! Freedom from the bonds that shackle us to this life of illusion – is that not a goal worth pursuing? But here again, you might want to be told – what exactly is this 'freedom' I am talking about? It seems suspicious if 'freedom' is tagged to 'discipline'! Surely, freedom means doing as one pleases; freedom is absence of all cares and responsibility; freedom is the opportunity to fulfill all of one's desires. Surely, all this is incompatible with discipline and 'spiritual practices' – whatever they may be!

Remember, we began by saying that *sadhana* is the means to an end: as I said earlier, this 'end' or 'goal' may vary from person to person: and the highest goal in Hindu thought is the goal of Liberation – freedom from worldly bonds, freedom from ignorance and illusion, freedom from the eternal cycle of birth-death-rebirth. The purpose of this human birth is to free ourselves from this vicious cycle. We may imagine that freedom is doing as we please; we may labour under the illusion that freedom is the ability to fulfill all our desires and satisfy all our sensual cravings: let us understand that all this is only going to shackle us deeper and deeper in bondage. True freedom is the capacity to do what we ought to do, to follow the path of goodness, truth and *dharma*, to be able to live with a pure heart, a clear conscience and an untainted mind. Freedom is breaking away from bad habits, addictions and wrong attitudes; freedom is conquering the lower self; freedom is the ability to rise to the highest level of consciousness and the purest level of thought that we, as human beings, are capable of. It is this level, this height of awareness that we reach when we follow Sri Krishna's profoundly simple, yet powerful advice in the Gita: "Whatever you do, whatever you eat or pray, do it as an offering unto Me!"

Sadhana is as simple as this: let all our thoughts and words and deeds be an offering unto the Lord.

Sister Shanti, Gurudev Sadhu Vaswani's spiritual daughter, once said to him, "Beloved Dada! I feel I cannot measure up to difficult spiritual practices. Is there any simple *sadhana* which I can perform easily and on which I can build my spiritual life?"

The Master said to her, "Even as the daisy turns to the sun, so you must turn to the Beloved! You must turn to God all the time!"

By sheer coincidence, a beautiful sunflower lay on the table. Pointing to it, the Master said to Shanti, "The sunflower is so named because it always faces the sun. It blooms with the rising sun, it turns its face towards the sun, following his path across the sky from east to west, and with the setting sun, it closes its many eyes! Be like the sunflower; it is the simplest *sadhana* that we can all undertake."

Is it not sad that we human beings are so fascinated by the glitter and glamour of the material world, that we live in forgetfulness of God and never really face Him? We forget to pray; we forget to thank Him for the countless blessings He has bestowed upon us; we forget to seek His blessings; we are swept away by the flood of worldly concerns and material desires.

Is this not ironic too, that the sun is millions of miles away from the earth, and yet the sunflower faces the sun persistently. As for God, He is here; He is everywhere; He is nearer than you believe; if truth were to be told, you don't have to go out to look for Him – for He is the Indweller within each one of us! All we have to do to 'find' Him, is look inward!

This, then, is *sadhana* at its simplest: it is to remember God – not once a day, not occasionally, not when you have a little free time – but to live and move in His presence, and feel His divine energy flowing through you!

But we devote our energy to worldly pursuits – seeking more power, seeking more pleasure, coveting worldly goods, yearning for bigger houses, bigger and faster cars, acquiring more wealth and influence – while we ignore the divine self that abides in us.

The Lord assures us in the Bhagavad Gita, that He will meet us on whatever path we choose to go to Him. This should be enough to assure us that there are no hard and fast prescriptions about the way to reach God, to attain Liberation. In fact, I would say that there are as many paths to self-realisation as there are the souls of men. The Gita points us towards three prominent paths. They are: (1) *Gnana Yoga;* (2) *Karma Yoga;* (3) *Bhakti Yoga.* Or, to put it even more simply, the first way is the way of self-enquiry, the second is the way of selfless service, and the third is the way of self-surrender.

However, it is advisable that each one of us should find out for ourselves, the path that suits us best. In this, as in many other aspects, the Hindu way of life gives us the kind of freedom that is rare in ancient religions.

I urge you, I earnestly beseech you, be aware that every breath of life is precious! Spend every moment, every minute in the consciousness that life is a gift from God. It is only through the human birth that we can achieve self-realisation, and return to God, to abide forever in *moksha,* our ultimate liberation.

I recall with gratitude a valuable lesson that Sadhu Vaswani taught me. One day the Master expressed a desire to have some fruits for breakfast. Eager to please him in every way I could, I asked him, "Gurudev, what fruit would you like to eat? Tell me and I will get it for you immediately!"

Sadhu Vaswani looked at me and smiled. "I think I would like to eat a few cherries," he said to me.

"I will get them immediately," I said and rushed off to the market in a tearing hurry. I searched high and low, but there were no cherries to be found for love or money. Every vendor gave me the same reply, "The season for cherries is over. You will not find them now."

Tired, dispirited and crestfallen, I returned to the Master. "Forgive me Gurudev," I said to him, "try as I might, I simply could not find any cherries."

Sadhu Vaswani said to me, "There is a season for everything. Once the season is over, we cannot avail of its benefits."

Come April, and mangoes make their appearance in India's colourful markets. In May and June we are hardly likely to find any fruit except mangoes on the streets and in the handcarts and stalls of the fruit vendors. Come July, the mangoes start to disappear. In August you will pay a heavy price for the rare mango; and in September, you cannot find mangoes no matter how hard you try. There is a time, a season for everything. If this season gets over, it will not come back again!

Well, you may wait for the next mango season or cherry season. But life does not easily give us a second chance. This life has been given to us for our spiritual evolution. And now is the time to begin. If this season is over it will not come back. Whatever is most important to us, must be done now. And the most important thing for all of us is the higher life that we seek. Therefore, we should start the work now. Now is the time. Now is the right season. There can be no postponement.

Therefore, Sant Kabir says, *"What you can do tomorrow, do it today. What you can do today, do it right now. For the holy ones tell us that this human birth is rare and precious."*

Any good thing that you wish to do tomorrow, do it today, don't postpone it, do it right now. Our time is limited and we should not fritter it away in false pursuits. This life of ours is rare and precious and not a moment should be wasted!

Ask Yourself

- Am I turning to outer activities to fill a void or vacuum that I feel within my heart?

- Why is it that I start out in the direction of my goals only to find myself off course soon?

- Do I feel the need to take some time to build a relationship with my own Higher Self?

- What am I seeking? Am I willing to discipline myself to achieve whatever it is that I am seeking?

- Do I feel lost in challenging times? Should I not create an anchor for myself?

- Do I work on improving myself constantly?

- Am I satisfied with material possessions? Or do I want emotional and spiritual stability?

- Am I willing to commit myself to a simple discipline to build an anchor for my life?

- Do I find myself setting goals and then not following through on them?

You Are Responsible for Your Own Salvation

Gurudev Sadhu Vaswani once narrated this parable to us: two men journeyed together through a jungle on a dark, starless night. One of them carried a lamp with him, and they moved on cautiously by its light. At midnight, they arrived at a point where their paths divided; from this point, each had to move on alone. The man with the lamp walked without fear. The other one was plunged into terror.

"If you wish to dispel the darkness around you, you must kindle the light," Sadhu Vaswani said to us. "And, remember, the Light is within you!"

How long can we look to others for lighting our way? How long can we depend on others to lead us forward in life? We have to take on the responsibility of our own life. We are accountable for our own Salvation.

At this point, some of you will probably intervene to say to me, "But we have our Guru! We have entrusted the responsibility of our salvation to him! Our future life is in his safe hands!"

To these friends, I would offer my hearty congratulations and good wishes: you are indeed fortunate that you have laid your life at the feet of a Guru, who, according to our scriptures, is much more than a father or mother to us: in fact, the equivalent of God upon this earth. But even then, my friends, your effort is not cancelled out. You have to cultivate and nourish the highest form of Guru *bhakti*, Guru *seva* and *sharanagati* (absolute surrender) to the Guru, if you wish to attain salvation through His grace. Believe me, that is also a *sadhana* of the highest order and rigour. I am sure you are not like the foolish disciple who went to his guru and demanded instant liberation at a price. For such a thing does not exist. *No pains, no gains* is especially true in this case!

My friends tell me that this is the age of outsourcing; BPOs are said to be the 'sunrise' industry; medical and legal records are outsourced; people no longer hire their own watchmen, domestic staff, gardeners or cleaners; an 'agency' takes care of everything for them. Even lunch and dinner for each day are outsourced by busy couples, or so I am told. Weddings and birthday parties are also outsourced to 'event' managers. The parents and the bride can arrive like guests at the wedding, while the agency takes care of everything!

Very nice indeed, for the agents and event managers. When people cannot manage their own affairs they provide livelihood to others.

I do realise the value of outsourcing: but I must point out that there are some things in life which we cannot outsource to others – and the chief among these is our own salvation. We have to work for it – and work very hard indeed, for there are no short cuts, no quick-fixes and no instant preparations and definitely, no paid service that can provide us this facility. This is why the *Paramacharya* of Kanchi once described the spiritual journey of man as the most selfless and the most exclusively 'selfish' of pursuits. Selfless because spirituality makes us rise above narrow, material concerns and selfish desires; selfish because we have to concentrate on the true self within us, to the exclusion of everything else and everyone else. You can pray for others; you can pay for others; but you cannot eat for them or sleep for them; nor can you offer your efforts for their liberation. That is a journey we must undertake on our own, like the two men in the jungle.

The fundamental value of Hinduism is the *dharma*, the *karma*, the duty, the devotion and the faith of the individual. We are not as 'organised' or as 'institutionalised' as other faiths. Nor is this a weakness. Our *Sanatana Dharma* has survived the onslaught of other religions, the ever-present threat of forced conversions and the internal attack from rationalists and atheists only because ours is a faith that is built on the individual's strength and faith and freedom to pursue the truth on his own.

In the Gita, after Lord Krishna has passed on many truths concerning life to his dear devoted disciple Arjuna, He finally tells him: "I have declared the truths to you; you must go and reflect upon these teachings and DO AS YOU CHOOSE!"

Hinduism uses no compulsion. You are free to enquire into its principles; you must be convinced of their truth, before you accept them. The laws of life are inviolable; they need no defenders, no patrons, no protectors. Each one of us must reach the Highest by his own free choice. There has never been any indoctrination in Hinduism.

A beautiful story is given to us in our ancient legends. A great *Rishi*, Yagnavalkya, comes to the palace of Raja Janaka, one of the greatest kings this land has known. Raja Janaka sits on a throne but his heart is the heart of a *fakir*, a saint, a holy man of God. This saintly ruler rejoices to see Rishi Yagnavalkya at his palace. He receives the sage, offers his *pranams*, and begs for a teaching at his holy feet.

Rishi Yagnavalkya begins to question the King. "Tell me, O King," says the Rishi, "What is the light whereby a man lives and moves and works and walks and finally to his home returns?"

Raja Janaka replies readily, "O Gurudeva, the light by which all men live and move, the light by which they work and walk and then to their homes return is the light of the Sun!"

Rishi Yagnavalkya smiles. "When the Sun has set, when its light has disappeared what is the light whereby men live and move and work and walk and then to their homes return?"

The King replies, "When the Sun has set, men must live and move, work and walk and then to their homes return by the light of the moon."

"And what if the sun and the moon have both disappeared?" queries the Rishi.

"Then, men must live and move and work and walk by the light of the fire," says the King.

"When the light of the sun, the moon and the fire have all gone out," continues the Rishi, "What is the light by which men can live and move and work and walk and to their homes return?"

The King is puzzled. He has no ready answer. He begs the Rishi to enlighten him.

Then it is that Rishi Yagnavalkya gives him the teaching – which I believe is the message of Hinduism to modern civilisation. The Rishi tells the King: "When all external light has gone out, when the sun does not shine, when the moon is not radiant and the fire is put out, there is still one Light that shines. It is the Light of the *atman*, the light of the spirit. It is this, which is the light of all lights. It is by this light that the sun shines, the moon is radiant and the fire is aglow. It is this light by which man must live and work and walk and to his eternal home return."

The Light of the *atman*, the Light of the Self, the Light of the Spirit – it was around this that our glorious culture was built in ancient India. This culture was known as *atmavidya* – the science of the spirit. For spirituality too, is a science, it concerns the discovery of the one self in all.

"To know others is wisdom, to know oneself is enlightenment," says Tao Tse Ching. Indeed, Socrates realised this truth too, in ancient Greece: that is why his constant refrain to his students was: *Know Thyself!*

In order to perceive this truth, in order to really know your true self, you must kindle the light within. This is the first and most essential step on the path of *sadhana*. This will inevitably lead you to the question: Who am I? What is the purpose of my existence here?

I would not be wrong, if I were to tell you that you rise or fall to the level of the purpose you have set for yourself! For you set your own goal: you create your own benchmark, and you reach it by your own efforts. If like the ancient decadents, you decide that the sole purpose of existence is to eat, drink and be merry until you drop dead, that is a goal which will not demand too much of effort on your part. If, like some ambitious businessman, you decide that the sole aim of your existence is to make millions and millions of dollars, your task is clear cut: you will require a great deal of business acumen and sound sense and the efforts to succeed in your business; if you make up your mind to settle for a steady 9 to 5 job and a quiet evening watching TV in your own living room, well then, you have your work cut out. But if you are looking for something that transcends all this, if you are looking for what we call self-realisation or God-realisation, you have set the highest possible goal that any human being can aspire to, and you must work very hard to achieve the goal. The goal is indeed worthy; and the efforts you put in to achieve it can only take you higher and higher up on the ladder of spiritual growth.

God has given you the gift of life; He has blessed you with a sound mind in a sound body, and these are instruments given to you to fulfill the purpose of your life. It is you who will decide what use they are to be put to.

There was a king who went out hunting and lost his way in the dense forest. Exhausted and famished, he knocked at the door of a broken down cottage which he found in the jungle. The occupant of the cottage was a humble hunter, who could not recognise the king; but he was kind and hospitable; he offered the visitor food and drink and a bed to sleep. The next morning, he led the visitor out of the jungle to the highway. Moved by his simplicity and kindness, the king revealed his identity to the poor man and said to him, "My friend, I am truly indebted to you for all that you have done for me at a time when I was lost and had no one to turn to for help. Here is some gold, which I offer you in gratitude. But, if ever you think I can be of help to you, do not hesitate to come to me. I promise you that I will do whatever I can to help you."

The hunter was a simple soul. He gratefully accepted the gold and returned home to his cottage in the forest. It did not occur to him that he now had 'powerful connections' and could exploit the king's promise to his own benefit. He continued to live his simple life in the forest, killing birds and small animals and selling their flesh in the villages around the area.

Years passed, and life grew increasingly tough for the hunter. One fine day, he recalled his tryst with the king and the promise made to him. With a little hope and a great deal of trepidation, he made his way to the palace, and waited outside the gates to catch a glimpse of the sovereign as he came out.

Sure enough, the king came out on his daily rounds and sure enough, he recognised the hunter as soon as his eyes fell on him! He greeted the poor man, invited him into the palace and ordered a sumptuous meal to be served to him. The hunter was ill at ease; he found the palace and its opulence overwhelming. He ate his meal and then stammered out the reason for his visit.

"O, Sire, I am growing old, and life is becoming harsh and difficult. If you could kindly provide a simple means of livelihood for me, I would be content to spend the rest of my days in comparative peace and quiet. I have been so bold as to come to you with this request, because your Highness promised me you would help me if ever I needed it".

The king was a compassionate and generous man. At a glance he understood the plight of the poor man, and his reluctance to accept royal favours. Gifts of gold and silver were not what he wanted. He sought a peaceful, stress-free life where he would not have to toil very hard to keep body and soul together.

"I have just the kind of work that would suit you," he said to the man. "Come with me, and I will show you what I have in mind for you."

He took the man to one of his favourite places in the kingdom: a carefully guarded and specially protected sandalwood forest, planted and grown by his ancestors. The forest lay in a secluded location, behind high fortress-like walls.

"This is a place that is very dear to me," he said to the poor man. "I am going to make you the watchman and guard of this forest. I will have a comfortable cottage built for you within the gates; you will receive a monthly wage and provisions from the royal granary. There are no thieves or poachers to fear. You will get the kind of quiet and peace that you are looking for. Are you willing to take up my offer?"

The poor man was speechless with gratitude. He thanked the king profusely, and in a very short while, he moved into his new home and began a new phase of his life.

He was given the uniform of the royal guardsmen; his cottage had been built by the king's own masons and carpenters. Every month, the royal treasury sent his wages to him; provisions and grains were supplied to him from the local state granary. He lacked nothing.

But even a life of indolence and inaction can prove difficult, though many of us may not realise this. Getting bored of walking around the sandalwood forest with nothing to do, the man hit upon an idea: why could he not chop some wood and sell it locally as he used to do in the past? It would be a little extra money on the side, and it would give him something to do, instead of walking around all day.

He began to chop the trees down, one by one. He was under

no pressure; it was not a hard existence any more. He worked leisurely and therefore more purposefully. He let it be known among the locals that he had firewood for sale; he did not even have to leave the forest; the villagers came to him in ones and twos and bought firewood. There was no pressure, no stress. He sold as much as he chopped.

Years passed. His royal duties had kept the king busy in state and military affairs. At long last, he remembered his old benefactor and his sandalwood forest. He decided to make a surprise visit to catch up with his guard and spend a little while in the forest.

You can imagine the shock that awaited him! Virtually the only thing left standing in the enclosed forest was the guard's cottage. The last sandalwood tree had been cut down and ready to be sold as logs for firewood. "My dear man," he said to the peasant, appalled at the sight, "what have you done with the forest that I entrusted to your care?"

I would not laugh contemptuously at the folly of the poor man. For I know that many of us are even more foolish, and throw away far greater treasures that are left at our disposal.

I have always pictured God greeting each one of us with love at the end of our earthly journey, and asking us just one simple question: "My dear child, what have you done with the life I gave you?"

You cannot, at that stage, refer God back to your secretary or manager or agent. You will be answerable yourself.

Ask Yourself

- Am I taking charge of my life?

- Does comfort impede my true goal?

- Is my life meaningful and purposeful? How can I live life fully?

- Do I feel responsible for my own actions?

- How do I take command right now in developing my own identification and self-worth?

- How can I consistently accomplish the goals I set along the path to living the life of my dreams?

- Am I happy? Do I need to change something in my life?

- Am I doing what I like or am I stuck in a groove?

- Am I a go-getter pursuing my goals or a mere spectator?

- Am I creating my own obstacles by believing them to be so?

- Exactly who or what is keeping me from taking command of my life?

The Goal of Life

Have you heard the beautiful *bhajan* 'Sukh Sagar Mein Aa-e-Kay, Mat Jaao Ray Pyasa Pyaray'? It is one of Sadhu Vaswani's immortal compositions. It is a *bhajan* that stirs within us an urge for the higher ideals of life. The song awakens the slumbering spirit; a sudden realisation dawns upon us: life is precious! Let us make the most of it. Let us not go back from this ocean of grace without tasting its sweet waters. Let us not go back exhausted. But let us drink the Divine Nectar and be blessed with bliss and peace.

This is the time of spiritual awakening, which puts you on the path of self growth, the path of *sadhana*. Walking on this path, you will feel that you are making your life meaningful and worthwhile; you will be happy to walk this path. But, you must know, no path is straight and smooth. It has its share of obstacles, steep gradients, unexpected curves and bends. So too with the path of life. A single trauma can shatter you, and make you feel helpless and ruined. Despair and melancholy constantly seem to wait on you. Troubles and anxieties surround you. At such times, you feel abandoned, your faith becomes vulnerable.

Gurudev Sadhu Vaswani often said to us, "You are not a weakling as some of you imagine yourself to be. In you is a hidden *Shakti*, an energy, that is of Eternity."

I once read the story of a beggar. He lived under a tree. He sat there through rain and sunshine, day and night, summer and winter. He was homeless and lived in abject poverty. He ate whatever people threw into his begging bowl. One day he fell ill; his body was racked by pain and fever. He had no money to buy medicine or to go to a doctor for treatment. He lay under the tree, ill and delirious until death released his soul from his wasted, emaciated body. A life of utter destitution had come to an end. The municipal workers accorded him the last dignity of a destitute funeral. He had left the world, unwept, unhonoured, unlamented.

A few days passed. The plot of land on which he had made his home was acquired by a construction company in order to build a commercial complex. Heavy equipment was brought to dig the ground and to lay the foundation for a huge building. When they had dug deep under the tree, the construction workers found a pot filled with silver and gold coins. This poor beggar had been literally sitting on a pot of gold; yet he had lived a life of utter deprivation. He was unaware of the treasure he was sitting on.

Are we not like that destitute beggar? An enormous treasure of *shakti* lies locked and hidden within us. But we go through life, without ever unfolding this *shakti*, without using it for own betterment. Little do we realise that we have the hidden potential that can transform our lives. There is a Power-house within us and we live in a state of permanent power failure.

We have passed through many lives. We have accumulated the *vasanas* of evil thoughts, words and deeds. We are imprisoned by the karmic bonds of our previous births, so much so that they have become the shackles of our present existence. We carry the yoke of negative *karmas* and we long to break free, like the pathetic fish caught in the snare of the trawler.

Don't let anyone tell you that escape from the snare is impossible. You can make your life anew. For man is not a creature of his destiny. He is the creator of his destiny.

If you wish to create your own destiny, you must be free of the burden of your past; you must erase the past through *Sadhana*, through the realisation of your true self. You must create a new space within, sow new thoughts of true liberation and freedom thereon. You must learn to meditate, you must go into silence; you must chant the Name of God within your heart. This will help you tap the latent power within you, it will open the reservoir of *shakti* that is deep inside your spirit. Once you experience this power, a new serenity, a vital energy will flow into your life. You will find this experience so uplifting, that you will overcome all the limitations of your physical existence, and rise above the restrictions of your external environment.

Let me repeat, you are not the pathetic weakling you take yourself to be. You are a spark of the Supreme Self. You are a child of God. His power and energy are yours. And you can harness this tremendous spiritual energy through *sadhana*.

Gurudev Sadhu Vaswani said to us: "The first step on the Path is awakening. The second is that of *Sadhana* or Self-discipline."

When the awakening has come, the seeker desires to discipline himself. And let us not forget, discipline is required both on the mental and physical plane. What is physical discipline for the aspirant who takes to *sadhana*? Let me dwell a little on this aspect.

The *Peace Chant* in the Upanishads begins with the words:

May my senses grow in perfection.

Do you find it strange – that the *rishi* asks for his senses to 'grow'? Strange indeed – but true. For asceticism is not always true mysticism.

Lacerations of the body, my Master taught us, will not lead us Godward: for the body, too, is an element in self-realisation. The natural is not cut off from the spiritual. Even Gautama Buddha learnt this valuable lesson before he finally attained Buddhahood or Enlightenment. The song of the maiden, "Tune the *sitar* neither low nor high," made him realise that excessive austerity and penance would lead to emaciation and exhaustion – but not necessarily the Enlightenment he sought!

We all know the story: he accepted the maiden's offering of sweetened milk, breaking his long fast of several days. Refreshed and rejuvenated with a new determination, he went back to his meditation; and the rest, as we say, is history!

Sadhana is disciplining of the senses; *sadhana* is also conquest over the senses; but it is not denial of the senses! The senses are gates of knowledge: and the *rishi* who prayed that his senses may grow in perfection was right. For seekers after higher life had to train their senses: how otherwise would they respond to higher vibrations? Let me share with you a beautiful verse from the *Mukunda Mala* of Sri Kulasekara Alwar –

That head is the loftiest which is white with dust from bowing down to Lord Krishna. Those eyes are the most beautiful which have abandoned darkness after they have seen Lord Hari. That intelligence is spotless, like the white glow of the moon, which concentrates on Lord Madhava. And that tongue rains down nectar which constantly glorifies Lord Narayana.

O tongue, praise the glories of Lord Kesava. O mind, worship the glorious Murari. O hands, serve the Lord Beloved of Lakshmi. O ears, hear the stories of Lord Achyuta. O eyes, gaze upon Sri Krishna. O feet, go to the temple of Lord Hari. O nose, smell the *tulasi* leaves on Lord Mukunda's feet. O head, bow down to Lord Narayana.

What is required is the purification of the senses, the disciplining of the senses and the dedication of the senses to the pursuit of the goal of existence.

There can be no growth in perfection without purity. The senses must be pure: whether they are over-fed or starved, the result is weakness. Maharishi Patanjali, too, asserts that *yoga* is not to be taught to those whose bodies are unsound. Therefore, the prayer: "May my senses grow in perfection!"

Sadhu Vaswani spoke of five aspects of our life which needed purification: and, it applies to all of us, and not just aspiring *sadhaks* or seekers!

1. The very first is *Vaak* – voice, utterance, sound, speech. Voice is the outer expression of thought. *Vaak* must be purified if you wish to grow in the perfect life.

Utter what you believe to be true. Speak out the truth – but not in bitterness. Purify your utterance by means of love. Do not wound or hurt the feelings of others.

Is it that someone's mode of worship does not appeal to you? Do not defile him as 'idolater' or 'infidel' or 'pagan'. Respect his views – but follow your own.

I wonder if you have noticed that how the *vaak*, the utterance of a saint, a realised soul, a pure and lofty master comes with a special meaning, a special music which goes straight to the heart? Such a one may speak in English, Hindi, Sindhi, German or Hebrew – but he speaks the language of love. Such *vaak* is pure. It has *shabda shakti* – so it touches the chord of the heart. The soul vibrates in response to this voice, and experiences joy.

Men of few words know the value of words as well as the worth of silence. Such men find it easy to practise the presence of God. They only utter those words which God puts into their mouth.

So, let us keep our *vaak* pure. Let us speak only that which is true, that which is pleasant and that which is useful.

2. Next to *vaak* is *prana*. *Prana* too must be purified, for it is our "life breath" – our respiration by which we live.

Many of us control speech, but are unable to control *prana*. When breath is properly controlled, drawn in and let out, it helps to keep body and mind healthy, relaxed and pure.

Prana is also the vital force that animates the universe, a primary energy with an enriching, invigorating quality. Thus, there is an indelible link between man and the universe, for the same life-force is manifest in both.

Most important of all, it is *prana* which links the body and the mind. Hence, its importance to mental, physical and spiritual well-being cannot be underestimated.

Pranayama is a unique, systematic, deep breathing exercise, associated with *yoga*. *Pranayama*, when practised in the proper method, enables the lungs to absorb optimum levels of oxygen so as to purify the blood, and thus ease the strain on the heart. Deep breathing can bring us immense benefits, including a stable mind, steady thinking, inner peace and a healthy life.

Pranayama is also a vital accompaniment of *dhyana* or meditation. As wise men from the East and West have repeatedly told us, the mind is the root cause of many diseases and ailments. With the purification of *prana*, we can attain the blessed gift of a healthy mind in a healthy body.

When *prana* is not controlled and purified, we get bad dreams. When we practise *pranayama*, even our dream-state, our subconscious life becomes good and pure.

3.   Next to *prana* is *chakshu* which is interpreted as sight. If only we realised how many sins are committed due to untrained, uncontrolled sight! A volume could be written on "modern degradation through sight" – degradation brought about by watching impure, unhealthy, unwholesome 'entertainment' and reading sensational novels.

A story is told to us of a Hindu devotee who plucked off his eyes and became sightless to escape sins of sight! Did not Jesus too echo the same idea, when he said, "If thy right eye offend thee, pluck it off?"

When the sense of sight is pure, no object is coveted and things are felt to be but passing apparitions of the One glory. Beauty becomes the glimpse of the Beloved who invites us, through the things that are seen, to the threshold of the Unseen, so that we may commune with Him!

4. Next comes *shrotrah*: hearing. This too, must be purified.

To listen to gossip, idle chatter, cruel criticism and malicious talk is to indulge in sin through hearing. The rule enjoined by our ancient sages is to hear only the good, the pure, the wholesome and the true.

And so, in books of the past we read how great was the value attached to hearing the Name of God. *Nama smarana* is one of the greatest sources of purification. So let us train ourselves, that we may hear, the Harmony, the Divine Music of the Universe. So let us purify ourselves, so that we may hear God's voice giving us His message in the heart within.

The singers of the *Upanishads* heard the *mantras*, the *deva vani* of the Divine! For us too, there is the call of the *Satguru*, the call of the Higher Self, which we can hear, when we rise above the assault of the senses.

5. And finally comes *baal*, which means 'vital sense' or 'bodily vigour'. One of the saddest things in modern life is the lack of recognition of the sanctity of the vital force, the creative force in us.

The Buddhists have a beautiful theory that *sanskaras* build up the man: and *sanskaras* are induced by man's contact with the environment. So it was in the ancient past, that the student of sacred knowledge (*Brahma Vidya*) and the seekers after higher life, were asked to observe *brahmacharya*. So were the senses trained so was the body built up, pure and strong.

One by one the senses must be disciplined, and thus prepared to walk the way of perfection.

The secret of self-discipline is purity: heart-purity, not purity of outer actions alone. We must cultivate purity of motive, thought and impulse: for purity is essential to the seeker on the path. As the *Upanishad* declares:

The knots of the heart must be snapped, the bars of desire must be broken, the heart must be pure.

God has given us a triple-treasure: 1) will; 2) thought; and 3) imagination. Let us keep them pure and undefiled. Let us submit ourselves to the best form of discipline – self-discipline. For without self-discipline, we will only drift as dead leaves in the autumn-wind!

Sadhu Vaswani once asked his Guru, "What is the greatest obstacle to the life of the Spirit?"

His Guru pointed out the differences between the life of flesh and the life of the spirit.

The life of the flesh is full of 'pleasure', of bodily sensations, of excitement and enjoyment: it is a life dear to the lowest 'self' in us. Eat, drink and be merry – is the motto of this life. And this life does not think of life beyond death.

The life of the Spirit is a battle with appetites and desires. And he who battles with desires, must often shed tears. Sometimes – perhaps often – he falls, but he rises again. It is a life of tremendous difficulties, a life of pain and struggle. But, it is also a life of search and quest. It is a life in which the cry of the heart even rises upward: it is a life of struggle, but it makes us heroic. And when the period of conflict is over, we are one with the pure, the holy, the divine! Can there be a higher goal than this? Can we ask for anything more?

In the life of flesh, we have pleasure, but darkness surrounds us. In the life of the Spirit, we struggle and fall: but we rise, again and again, until, at last, we touch the divine! This is what *sadhana* is all about.

"This is the life you must aspire to," the Guru said to Sadhu Vaswani. "The path is often thorny, and as you tread the path, your feet may bleed – but in your heart will bloom flowers of beauty, and your face will shine as the lily or lotus in the lake."

Ask Yourself

- What is my life's calling?

- How did I get to where I am now? Where do I want to go from here?

- What do I want out of life?

- Do I know myself as well as I think I do?

- Where am I heading in life?

- When I am old, what will I want to say about my life?

- Do I realise the value and importance of the human birth that has been bestowed upon me?

- Do I often criticise or hurt others?

- Do I talk sweetly and lovingly to people around me?

- Do I choose purposefully what I want to do with each moment?

- Do I want to unlock my hidden potential?

Sadhana = self-discipline.

Sadhana is For Everyone

Many people are apt to imagine that *sadhana, abhyasa, bhakti* and *dhyana* are practices meant exclusively for people who have renounced worldly life – or at least, for people who have withdrawn from worldly concerns. Nothing can be farther from the truth than this blithe but false assertion. The kind of *sadhana* that I have been talking to you about is nothing but self-discipline. Who is it who can say that they do not need self-discipline in their lives?

There is another important point that I must emphasise before we proceed further. Although *sadhana* is aimed at cultivating the spirit and enhancing spiritual health and spiritual growth, it has the most beneficial and positive effect upon our external life, the life of transaction with our fellow human beings. I will also go one step further and say this: if your *sadhana* does not make you a better human being, a better person to deal with, a kinder, more mature, more understanding person in your relationships, and a more focused, more concentrated, more effective person at work, your *sadhana* has not really been successful.

A friend to whom I made this observation was highly skeptical about it. "Surely, Dada, *sadhana* is an exclusively spiritual pursuit," he objected. "We cannot expect it to make us better salesmen, better managers or better businessmen. As I understand it, *sadhana* is not a worldly pursuit at all."

I smiled and said to him, "How easily we make the division between worldly and unworldly. How firmly we insist on keeping the spiritual and the material world apart. I am not for such exclusivity as you advocate. I believe the infusion of spirituality in all our worldly activities can only make us more successful, more human and more peaceful in all that we do."

Let me explain: discipline is akin to cleanliness and order. Would you work at a desk that is cluttered with files and papers and objects that have neither been dusted nor put away in their proper places? Or would you prefer to begin work each morning at a desk which has been cleared away by you the previous evening and has been wiped and dusted early in the morning and awaits the day's work?

Would you like to live in a house that is cluttered, filled with old disused furniture and unwanted stuff that has not been thrown away for ten years, ill-maintained, with leaks in the kitchen and bathroom, wiring faults in the electric line and infested with pests? Or would you prefer to live in a clean and tidy house which is swept and dusted and well maintained, in which everything is in its right place?

Discipline in your personal life touches all aspects of your life. The enhancement of your spiritual quotient can only have a beneficial influence on your personal and professional life.

I have said this to you repeatedly, the human life is a great blessing; and the human personality, that wonderful complex of body, mind and spirit, is a truly invaluable gift. There is no accomplishment, no achievement that is not possible to us if we use this gift well. Self-discipline or *sadhana* is nothing but the proper maintenance and the right utilisation of this great gift.

Thus, self-discipline is a way of enhancing the value of your life. It brings about peace, harmony, joy, perfection and self-fulfillment in your life. We should not look upon self-discipline as something that is imposed on us from the outside, as something that we are compelled to practise against our will; but rather, as something that is desirable, essential and in the best interests of us and our loved ones.

Self-control and self-discipline are pre-requisites to success not only on the spiritual plane, but in all activities we undertake.

- A young lady who is keen to lose weight, prescribes certain disciplines to herself: she avoids high-calorie foods even if they are tempting to her palate; she willingly submits herself to a strict regimen of exercise until the desired weight loss is accomplished.

- A student who is set on clearing exams like GATE, GMAT or CAT goes through hours and hours of rigorous preparations everyday; he joins special coaching classes; he learns to become more analytical and more logical in his approach; he gives up trivial pursuits like roaming around with friends and watching TV until his chosen goal is accomplished.

- A budding entrepreneur who has just started off on a new business venture practises severe restraint in personal spending; he does not leave his work undone to rush home at the stroke of five o'clock; he dedicates time and effort to cross hurdles one by one and move steadily towards his goal.

- A young mother considers no sacrifice too high to make for her child. She sets aside all personal needs, at times turns her back on a lucrative career, gives second place to her personal ambitions and focuses all her attention, time and effort on her child, determined to give the child the best that she is capable of.

Tell me, dear friends, are not all these achievements tied up with self-discipline and focused effort? Discipline of mind, body and spirit is the key to success in all spheres of our lives. At the highest level, it takes us close to God – and which of us can dismiss that goal as unnecessary or worthless?

"Seek ye first the kingdom of heaven, and all these things shall be added unto you!" were Jesus's words to us. Spirituality is pursuit of the highest goal of life, permanent residence in the kingdom of God; but the pursuit of this goal on this earth-plane brings with it, countless gifts at the personal level, which makes life upon earth a blessing to us and others.

Self-discipline strengthens our will-power and enables us to become masters of our senses and our activities. It increases our self-confidence and enables us to realise that we are not pathetic weaklings and slaves to the senses and passions; it makes us aware that we are architects of our own destiny. It gives us the conviction that our ideals and aims are worth pursuing. It enables us to cultivate virtues like perseverance, hard work, patience and dedication – and anyone will tell you that these are sterling qualities that are as essential to worldly success as they are to spiritual pursuits.

I do not wish to sound harsh, but it is only at a very low level of intelligence and perception that we can imagine that sensual pleasures and material achievements are the highest goals worth pursuing in life. As we become more mature, as we learn to think at a more advanced level, as we realise the value of this life and the goal we must ultimately reach, self-discipline becomes spontaneous with us. True, our efforts must be redoubled, our perseverance strengthened at every step; but the goal we have set for ourselves, the ideals we hold dear become precious to us, and self-discipline becomes second nature to us!

Ask any Olympic athlete about his/her self-discipline; you are not likely to hear a litany of complaints on how tough it was and a wail of moaning on all the sacrifices that had to be made. Rather, the successful athlete will only say how worthwhile all of it was, and how wonderful it was to achieve the goal. Success is sweet, and self-discipline becomes sweeter and more spontaneous when the goal is always retained in mind.

Of course, to those who are not serious about their goal, self-discipline is a pain, a tough chore, a severe restraint. But, when you are in tune with your highest ideals, when you realise the worth of pursuing those ideals, discipline becomes automatic in your life; as they say, it becomes second nature with you. External compulsions and force are not necessary for you; you become self-motivated and self-discipline becomes spontaneous, allowing you to become more efficient, more effective, more energetic and empowered to achieve your dreams and accomplish great things for yourself and others!

Ask Yourself

- What is my attitude to discipline in any form?

- Am I willing to sacrifice small pleasures to attain higher goals?

- How do I feel about myself? Why?

- How important are my goals and dreams to me? Am I willing to work towards them?

- Do I connect *sadhana* to spirituality alone?

- What do my thoughts and behaviour express?

- What does self-discipline mean to me?

Sadhana for Children

Gurudev Sadhu Vaswani often said to us: "Our children are our greatest treasure! We must give them time, attention and love without which no child can grow in the right way. We must never, ever neglect their interest."

Anything that we can say on *sadhana* for children, must perforce, begin with the parents. For it is the parents who must take full responsibility for shaping and moulding the plastic minds of the children in their formative years.

I know many parents today are involved in the task of making their children's future secure and comfortable. To this end, they work hard and invest in insurance schemes and real estate and mutual funds; they buy up movable and immovable assets; over and above all this, they reach out beyond all available means to give their children the best education possible.

While I appreciate this, I must nevertheless add that the greatest gift they can bestow on their children is to inculcate self-discipline in them when they are still young and free from peer pressure and their minds are receptive. I definitely believe that this is the key to success in life.

Here is a story that aptly illustrates this point.

The grand concert came to a close and the audience stood up

spontaneously to give a standing ovation to the violin maestro whose solo performance had been the highlight of the evening. Thunderous applause filled the concert hall. The maestro who had played one of the most powerful violin concertos of Vivaldi, came forward to take a bow and accept the cheers of the audience. Eagerly, a woman made her way to the stage in hope of expressing her admiration to this great artist. Threading her way through the crowd, she finally reached him. Shaking his hand, she said exuberantly, 'Oh, I'd give my life if I could play like that!'

The maestro promptly responded, "Madam, that is exactly what I have done."

In professional success, as in the search for self-realisation, there is no alternative to hard work and discipline.

I am afraid that many parents regard discipline as something that must be left to their children's schools and teachers, while they, as parents, should simply indulge their children's whims and fancies. Many children are brought up thinking that they deserve to get all that they want and all that they expect from their indulgent parents. They insist on getting what they want as and when they want it. In many cases, they are not willing to work for it, nor wait patiently for it. In short, they are utterly lacking in self-discipline.

I recall the story of a young man in France. Having committed a heinous crime, he was sentenced to hard labour for ten years. He received his sentence calmly. But, as he was being led away by the police, he turned towards the people present in court, and shouted aloud so that everyone could hear him: "I have nothing against the judges – for they have dealt with me justly. I have nothing against the police – for they have done their duty. However, I can never forgive two persons in this courtroom – my father and my mother!"

People listened to him, shocked beyond words, too stunned to react.

"They are responsible for my present condition," he continued. "They paid no attention to my upbringing. They did not take care of the company I moved in; they never bothered to find out who my friends were. True, they gave me money to spend – but did not bother to find out what I spent it on. They did not object when I gambled, took to drinking and visited houses of ill-repute. And so here I am – full of vice and crime. The fault is theirs but I pay the price for it, sentenced to hard labour in prison, to be branded as a convict for life."

Harsh words! But the young man's bitterness cloaks the truth that many parents do not seem to realise their responsibilities towards their children. So it was that William Penn said: "Men are generally more careful of the breed of their horses and dogs than of their children."

Dr. Cordelia Fine, an adolescent psychology expert, suggests that parents must start very early to 'build the moral muscle' of their children. Strengthening their moral fibre and their will power can work wonders for children – from good grades to healthy habits and a clean lifestyle.

Parents must create an environment of care, love and warmth in the home, where discipline is a way of life accepted by all the members of the family. This does not mean taking away the children's freedom; rather, it is allowing them to realise that freedom and responsibility go hand in hand. I do not think it is good for a teenager to have his own way all the time. Your love for him must not come in the way of training him and inculcating discipline in him.

Many parents are reluctant even to reprimand their children, leave alone punish them for any wrong-doing. This is definitely not in the children's interest. If you love your children deeply, you will see to it that they understand the sincerity of your intentions and respond to your corrective measures positively.

If children are to seek perfection through self-discipline, the parents must have the following basic traits:

1. They must have higher aspirations themselves and realise the value of spiritual growth.

2. They must be in perfect understanding and harmony with each other.

3. They must not seek after material possessions and trivial pursuits and entertainments.

4. They must not allow the children to pursue their whims and desires indiscriminately. Allowing the children to watch TV at all times is one such indiscriminate indulgence. Also, excessive pocket money, lavish gifts and junk food should be avoided.

5. Parents must participate in their children's leisure activities and involve themselves in the life of the children at all levels. Paid caretakers, mechanised entertainment and luxurious holidays can never substitute for personal care and genuine affection.

The question then arises: "How should parents raise their children?"

Regular, daily prayer at home can play a vital role in shaping the character of your children. Other spiritual practices can include the following:

• Meditation and yoga, taught under the guidance of a special teacher trained to impart them to children

• Repetition of the Name Divine

• Reading the scriptures and the *bani* of great ones

• Study of great *puranas* like the *Ramayana* and *Mahabharata*

• Practise of *likhit japa* – writing of the Name Divine

Many of my friends who live abroad also request the Sadhu Vaswani Mission to organise special camps, weekend retreats and summer schools for children where they can imbibe the values and ideals of our Hindu culture.

When prayer becomes a part of your child's life, it lays down the spiritual foundation for his wholesome development. When you teach your child to cultivate absolute faith in God, you are also teaching him to tackle all problems – physical, emotional and spiritual – in the best possible way.

The home is a door to the kingdom of God, the kingdom of true happiness. Let all the members of the family gather together, at a prayer meeting – even if it be for ten to fifteen minutes. This will give a new tone to the home. At a prominent place in your home, keep a big, beautiful picture of some great one – Krishna or Rama, Buddha or Jesus, Zoroaster or Guru Nanak, Mira or Mahavira, Baha'u'llah or Kabir or a saint of humanity – to whom you feel drawn. Whenever you or the children leave the house or enter it, bow down to the picture and offer a small prayer.

It is crucial for children to be taught the power and value of silence. Living in this fast, noisy age, children are often full of restless energy. It is vital that we teach them to sit still and observe silence for at least a few moments. This is where *satsang* becomes essential. Initiating children into the *satsang* at an early age is, I think, a highly desirable practice. Sitting in prayer at the *satsang* will become an effective way of calming them down, and helping them to overcome their restless nature.

If children could be taught to surrender themselves to the grace of God and the Guru, it would be the best thing that could happen to them. Let them realise that God and the Guru are always at hand to protect them, guard them, and prevent them from yielding to evil and temptation. Teach them to remember their God and Guru first thing, when they awaken, and last thing, before they fall asleep. They should be taught also, to repeat the Name of God and their supplication to the Guru, during the course of the day. This will help them do well in their studies, it will give them better concentration and focus, it will guard them from all danger and evil.

Help your children to develop morals and values – not by lecturing to them or enforcing rules on them, but by making them aware of what is right and wrong, and about acceptable and unacceptable behaviour.

This is easier said than done. But you can inculcate values in the children by :

1. Laying down rules that are consistent and clear – not confusing and contradictory.

2. Talking to children about society, politics, religion and spirituality in a way that appeals to them. For instance, a recent event or development could be discussed by the family, so that children draw the right lessons from the same.

3. Encouraging children to express their choices and attitudes to these issues, and trying to understand their reasons for their opinions.

4. Involving the children in constructive community activities such as social service, peace rallies and public discourses by eminent spiritual leaders so that they are exposed to a broader, more selfless view of life. Asking for their help and contribution in family events and community activities.

5. Making them responsible and accountable for their actions, and helping them to realise the consequences of their own actions. If they have made a wrong decision or a poor choice, they must be held accountable, and allowed to experience the bad effects, so that they take the corrective measures in a spirit of awareness and understanding. Allowing them to take responsibility for decision-making and leadership wherever possible.

6. Being good, fair, consistent parents—rather than trying to spoil your child, and doing all you can to win his favour. Your role is to be a true friend, guide and guardian to the youngster— not someone who wants to please them and win a popularity contest. Being affectionate, caring parents – but also firm and

fair-minded at the same time.

7. Practising what you preach. I have said earlier, children learn far more from your life and from your behaviour, than from your verbal instructions.

Parenting is not only one of greatest pleasures of your life – it is also an onerous responsibility, involving psychology, ethics, human resource management, spirituality, morals and religion. Whatever I have outlined above are not to be taken as rigid rules, but they can help you induct your children, from their impressionable years, on the path of spiritual growth.

Let me conclude by saying to you, your children look up to you for a sense of security, identity and belonging. The world we live in is changing so fast, that they are exposed to powerful, sometimes negative influences from outside. The only weapon you have to fight these negative influences is your love – therefore, make your child feel loved, cherished and secure. Express your love in as many ways as you can, as often as you can. Let your discipline and control become expressions of your love and concern – rather than being merely negative feedback and criticism. Give them your unstinted praise and appreciation when they deserve it. Treat them as young adults and as responsible members of the family unit. You will find that your children bloom and flower into mature, sensible adults under your loving care.

Seven Steps To Help Children on the Path

(Suggestions for parents)

1. Give your children a happy, wholesome, harmonious atmosphere in the home. The home is the door to the kingdom of God, and your child's spiritual growth starts right here.

2. In their formative years, children must come to look upon their parents as their best friends. Therefore, cultivate deep affection and closeness to your children.

3. Teach children to grow in the spirit of selflessness by training them to share what they have with the less fortunate ones. Tell them of Sri Krishna's injunction in the Gita: "He who cooks food for himself alone is a thief."

4. Let the family pray together, at an appointed time everyday, even if it be for ten to fifteen minutes. This will give a new tone and a new zest to family life.

5. Enrol your children in classes and group activities where children might get to know the culture and ideals of their Faith. Let them grow in love for Indian traditions and culture, so that they know where their roots are.

6. To enhance their faith, narrate to them stories from the great epics and *puranas,* incidents from the lives of the *avataras,* saints and spiritual leaders. This will make them aware of the great spiritual *shakti* that operates in the universe.

7. From time to time, arrange a special service programme or activity in which children can involve themselves. For example, spend a child's birthday at an orphanage or a home for handicapped children, where the child can distribute food and gifts to the other children and spend some time playing with them. This helps children grow in the spirit of compassion.

Ask Yourself

- Am I a good role model for my kids?

- What is the greatest gift that I can give my children to aid their success in life?

- Do I let my love for my children come in the way of training or disciplining them?

- Do we pray together as a family?

- Are my children aware of what is right and what is wrong?

- Do I have open and honest discussions with my children to discern their thought process?

Sadhana for Teenagers

Eleanor Roosevelt, whom I regard as a very wise woman, once remarked, "Beautiful *young* people are accidents of nature, but beautiful old people are works of art." I would like to modify her statement by saying: beautiful *young* people who learn the secret of self-discipline always turn out to be beautiful adults and beautiful human beings all their lives.

The teenage years are a time of transition from childhood into adulthood. This is also a period of intense growth, not only physically but morally and intellectually. This is why the teenagers' considerable energy and intelligence must be channelised into positive, constructive activities that can help them evolve into successful, happy, fulfilled human beings in later life.

Despite a few negative perceptions about teenagers, we may see that many of them are very often energetic, thoughtful, helpful to others and idealistic; they are less prone to selfishness and less intent on moneymaking; they nourish high hopes about themselves and the world they live in; they have a deep interest in what is fair and right. So, although it can be a period of conflict between parent and child, the teen years are also a time to help children grow into the distinct individuals they will become. Thus, teenage power is a much used word these days. Indeed, those golden years from thirteen to nineteen are unforgettable to us. It is the age when we believe that everything is possible to us; it is the age when the world seems to be our oyster; it is the age of dreams and high ambitions and lofty goals and all of these actually seem within grasping distance!

Psychologists, alas, have a very different view: they view the 'adolescent years' as a troubled time for teenagers and their parents. The teenager is insecure about his growth and appearance. He is desperately seeking to find his own identity. Taller, slimmer, more good looking, more athletic, more talented peers make him feel inferior. Negative feelings and a low self-image haunt many young teenagers. Some of them have difficulty making friends and handling social contacts. The dreaded 'generation gap' sets in, and teenagers often grow away from their parents, and sometimes pass through periods of depression and turmoil. Therefore, it is understandable that it is a time of confusion and upheaval for many families.

But there is no such thing as the stereotypical teenager with adolescent problems and the permanently rebellious attitude. The primary goal of the teen years is the desire to achieve independence. In order to attain this goal, some teens may start pulling away from their parents – especially the parent whom they're the closest to. As teens mature, they also learn to think more objectively, abstractly and rationally. This is the crucial stage when they are forming their own moral code.

Sometime ago, I received an American newspaper carrying the headline: *School-gang violence is now near-epidemic: vandalism, arson, murder, burglary.* The paper quoted an official of the Los Angeles Country Board of Supervisors, who said: "We *have* to return to discipline. Without discipline in the home, we are not going to have it in the schools or in the streets. We must arouse public opinion for a change." The paper also reported how three teenagers – aged fourteen, fifteen and seventeen – had killed a man and a woman just to steal from them the paltry sums of three dollars and ten dollars.

In subsequent years, the world was shocked to hear of school boys or college students just opening fire on their friends and teachers in the campus, causing needless bloodshed and loss of lives – apparently, with no reason.

You might respond to this by saying, "But Dada, surely we have also heard that in India too, a harsh word from the teacher, or a stern beating by the headmaster, have led some sensitive young students to commit suicide! Is not such 'discipline' terrible?"

Let me explain to you – discipline is necessary; discipline is vital. But, discipline must not be confounded with suppression or oppression.

I am reminded of an amusing anecdote. There was a teenage boy. When someone asked what his name was, he answered, "Haresh Don't".

"Don't?" said the visitor. "That's a strange surname. Are you sure you are Haresh *Don't*?"

"Sure, I'm sure," said the boy solemnly. "Everytime I want to play in the house, mama says, 'Haresh, don't!'. Everytime I laugh loudly, papa says, 'Haresh, don't!'. Everytime I run down the stairs, someone says, 'Haresh, don't!'. So my name is really Haresh Don't."

This is not the kind of discipline I am talking about. We must treat our teenagers like the intelligent beings that they are. We must teach them about the values that are essential to them; we must tell them about the gift of human life and explain to them that discipline is needed to reach life's goals.

One of the most important tasks for all adolescents is learning to master those skills and cultivate those habits and attitudes that will help them manage their own lives successfully and make positive, healthy choices. Parents and teachers must help them develop this sense of self-governance, responsibility, independence, and decision-making, by ensuring that their energies are directed towards the right goals. But discipline and control must not undermine the teenagers' sense of autonomy – the awareness and the responsibility of being in charge of their lives.

How do we describe/evaluate our own moral standards? How do we choose the ideals and values by which we wish to live? It is not quite correct to assume that a person's values are formed during childhood – and do not change after that. Psychological research as well as personal experience shows us that as people mature and evolve, they *change* their values in very deep and profound ways. As we grow spiritually and emotionally, we acquire the ability to think deeply on issues that are of lasting importance to us.

As children, we are simply told what is right and what is wrong. As adolescents, we begin to *internalise* these moral standards. We do what is right because our 'group' expects it of us – group here referring to our family, friend's circle, peer groups and so on. But we also begin to acquire the capacity to reflect on, analyse and evaluate the moral standards, values and ideals bequeathed to us. The transformation of the adolescent into a mature adult is a crucial stage in the life of every individual. This is why I feel that teenagers must take to *sadhana* in the measure possible to them.

I have said to my friends repeatedly, life is a matter of choices that we make. At every step, every round of life, we make a choice between good and evil, between what is easy and difficult, between right and wrong, between what is practical and useful and what is ideal and desirable. This is the good old choice between *preya* and *shreya*! Teenagers are especially vulnerable to the temptation of *preya* – the smooth and easy path that leads us to self-indulgence and a life of slavery to the senses. Their youth, their immaturity and their inexperience makes them vulnerable to make the wrong choice. How can they guard themselves against this?

It was a wise man who said: "An educational system isn't worth a great deal if it teaches young people how to make a living but doesn't teach them how to make a life."

In this, as in other matters, our ancient culture shows us the way.

In the *ashramas* of ancient India, the *rishis* taught their disciples the technique of imbibing the great truths and values essential for righteous living through three crucial stages: *shravana, manana* and *nidhyasana.* It is good for our teenagers to follow the same tried and tested path today.

The first stage is *shravana* – which means hearing. We must hear good things; we must hear good teachings; we must hear spiritual discourses. But hearing is not enough. We must not stop there. *Shravana* in modern language also refers to reading. Many of us recite from the scriptures. Some people actually know the Bhagavad Gita by heart. They recite the whole of the Gita. But mechanical recitation of the scripture will not take us very far.

Therefore, the *rishis* talk of the second step, which is *manana.* *Manana* means reflection; it means thinking upon what we have heard and read. When you ponder upon what you have heard, doubts are likely to awaken within your heart. These doubts should be placed at the feet of a spiritual elder or a Guru. He may be able to clear these doubts and show you the way. But *manana* is a vital stage – you must reflect upon the teachings.

The third step is the most essential – for you cannot stop with reflection. The third step must be taken by everyone who wishes to tread the path of *sadhana* – this third or crucial step is *nidhyasana* or assimilation. You must assimilate the teachings you have been given in your daily life. Your life must bear witness to the great teachings you have heard, reflected upon and finally, absorbed. You must become the very picture of the great truths that you have assimilated.

Life is not just about finding yourself; it is about creating yourself for the life that you are meant to live.

Here are a few simple suggestions for my teenage friends to practise *sadhana:*

1. Get to know God and love Him. If He is kept out of your 'secular' curriculum in school or college, attend special classes for getting to fill the vacuum. When you make God a reality in your life, you will grow in those true qualities of character without which life has no meaning or significance. God is Light! Without this awareness, the logical intellect, and the selfish, self-seeking mind will only lead you on the path of materialism, which ends in darkness. But awareness of God, awareness of Light will lead you towards spiritual unfoldment – the highest goal of all education.

2. Do not look for short-cuts, quick fixes and easy solutions. For, like the oak tree, the mind and character take time to shape up and grow. And we require all eternity to attain to perfection.

3. Avoid self-indulgence and excessive dependence on physical comforts. Gurudev Sadhu Vaswani said: "I am afraid many of our students want comfort, ease, enjoyment. I am afraid many of them sleep too much. Too much sleep only dulls the brain. Education is self-discipline. Modern students only run after fashion and folly – after *bhoga.* Students must learn to discipline themselves."

4. Never ever shirk your duty. An over-confident teenager once argued with me that Sri Krishna tells us in the Gita, that the battle must be fought and won by fair means or foul. I was appalled at this misinterpretation and the force of conviction with which it was uttered. Such ethical confusion arises only when values are not upheld. We live in a world of moral turpitude, because people are only aware of their *rights,* and not of their duties. What the Gita teaches us, in essence, is to do our duty, without expecting anything in return.

5. If I had a million tongues, with each one of them I would appeal to my young friends who are going to be tomorrow's leaders and opinion makers – Seek not power! Seek service!

Let us do as much good as we can, in as many ways as we can, on as many occasions as we can, and as long as we can.

"What do we live for if not to make the world less difficult for each other!" asks the famous writer and novelist, George Eliot. I am afraid our career oriented, job-driven education is making our youth self-centred, constricting them to lead narrow, selfish lives. But it is only in compassionate, altruistic living that we can discover the best that we are capable of.

Therefore, let me say to my young friends: give of yourself, give of your time, talents and energies to lighten the loads of the weary and the heavy-laden.

6. Do your duty *and a little more!* Therefore, grow beyond responsible citizenship to become good human beings. You must realise that the opposite of love is not hatred, but *apathy* or indifference – indifference, insensitivity to the needs of others. Can you read? Then read to a blind student. Can you write? Then write a letter, fill a form for someone who is not so lucky as you are. If you are not very hungry, share your food with someone who is. If you are at peace with yourself, reach out to those who are in pain, and disturbed by their suffering. All of us have something to give. Let us give what we can to others – our time, our effort, our understanding, our love, our concern, our sympathy, our smiles. Let us give with love and compassion.

Even if one person is comforted by your words; even if one person's broken heart is healed by your understanding; even if someone's misery is wiped out by your kindness – you have made a difference.

7. Aspire to be a truly cultured individual. And know this – that self-discipline and self-control are the key to understanding the culture that is unique to the land of the Vedas. Western culture lays emphasis on power and material acquisitions; it is the essence of Indian culture to value the spirit – the eternal, imperishable *atman* – above all else. This is why you will find common people bowing to leaders, millionaires, celebrities in the West, while in

India, leaders, millionaires and common public alike bow down in reverence to men and women who have renounced the world and live a life of contemplation and reflection.

When you are educated in the spirit of the true Indian culture, you will take pride in being Indian. You will turn your back on the slavish habit of blindly imitating the West. In fact, Sadhu Vaswani taught us that slavishness, imitation, intolerance, aggressiveness, narrowness and coarseness are sins against culture; while inner independence, simplicity, refinement, large-mindedness, humility, free activity, rich vital idealism – are all true marks of a cultured individual.

8. Man becomes what he thinks, taught our ancient *rishis*. Therefore it is not theory, not a set of definitions and maxims, but exemplary role-models, great figures who can shape your lives. And India has given us so many of these great souls, radiant with the light of lofty ideals – *rishis* and sages, poets and prophets, heroes and holy men, singers of the spirit, men of action and devotion, men and women of dedicated lives – from Yagnavalkya, Sukha, Maitreyi and Arjuna, to the later ones, Buddha and Mahavira, Kabir and Guru Nanak, Chatrapati Shivaji, Lokamanya Tilak, Ramakrishna Paramahansa, Swami Vivekananda, Mahatma Gandhi and Sadhu Vaswani. Choose any one of them as a role model. Read as much as you can about him; imbibe his teachings; and put at least one teaching into practice everyday of your life. You will be amazed at the transformation this brings about in your life.

9. *Vidya dadati vinayam* – so our scriptures teach us. True knowledge, true scholarship is humility. Do not be content with becoming sharp and shrewd, clever, aggressive and competitive; do not be motivated only by self-interest; look upon the world with reverence. Respect your teachers and parents.

10. Determine to live a life that is clean, honest and incorruptible; have the courage to stand up for what is right, and to heed the still, clear voice of your conscience at all times.

Let me close this chapter with the powerful words of Gurudev Sadhu Vaswani which still echo in my heart like the majestic sounds of a temple bell.

O child of Beloved Bharata! Look around you and see that the world is sad, is broken, is torn with tragedy, is smitten with suffering. Living in such a world, you must learn to share the good things of life that have been bestowed upon you; you must share them with those that are in need. Remember, you cannot be happy when so many around you are unhappy. If you would be happy, go and make others happy. The happiness that you give others will come back to you, such is the law. For happiness moves in a circle.

Here is a list of questions you can ask yourself. They were written for a teenagers' website by a 16 year old Nigerian youngster.

What are the changes I want to make to my world?

What influence can I have on people's lives?

What is my mission?

What is my goal?

What is my choice (life or death)?

What have I been created for?

What is my primary assignment?

Who are my mentors?

What impact am I going to leave on people's lives?

What will people remember me for?

What is the legacy I want to leave for my children?

My future awaits me and am I preparing for it?

How disciplined am I to my education and life?

If I am lucky and receive opportunities will I use them?

How do I create opportunities for other people?

Three Steps On The Path For Teenagers

1. Every morning, as you wake up, think of some *sutra* (small text) from the Sacred Books and repeat it to yourself again and again. As the day advances, from time to time, detach yourself from work for a brief minute or two and repeat the *sutra*. Imagine that the *sutra* permeates your entire being and renews you physically, mentally and spiritually. I have found the following very helpful – "Thy will be done, O Lord!" "Thou knowest best what is good for each one of us!" "Thy works are the works of mercy!" "The Lord is my strength, my support and stay!" "In Thy will is the peace I seek!"

2. In the face of difficulty and disaster, do not feel confused. But lift up your heart to Him and think of Him as a Loving Mother and of yourself as a little child sitting on Her Lap. Then sing to yourself a song on:

Mother mine! Mother Divine!
He on whom is Thy protecting Hand –
Him no sorrow can strike!

3. Steer yourself clear of all thoughts of lust, hatred and greed. They stimulate the lower self and lead to excitement which will not let us to be still in God.

Gradually, this stillness will deepen, though the very first experience of it gives such immense joy that it cannot be expressed in words. The stillness will grow more and more intense until, one blessed day, we shall be completely absorbed in God and entirely at one with His divine will which is perfect – not only for us but for all men and birds and beasts, for all creation.

Ask Yourself

- Am I desperately seeking to find my own identity?

- Am I happy with the choices I have made in my life so far?

- Do I shirk my duties and responsibilities?

- Am I insecure about myself?

- Am I willing to discipline myself to achieve my goals and dreams?

- Who is my role model?

- Do I equate material possession with happiness?

Sadhana for Businessmen and Professionals

Sometime ago, a friend who is a successful businessman approached me with a little diffidence, and asked me, "There is a deep yearning in me to explore my inner self and to commune with the inner voice; is it possible for someone like me to take to a life of *sadhana*? Which path would be the right one for me to follow? Can you recommend a method which I can follow in the midst of all my business responsibilities and obligations?"

I said to him, "Dear brother, you are a householder and a businessman. The best thing for you would be to experience the presence of God in whatever work you do. Do your work honestly, refrain from all evil actions; avoid malice and gossip; bear witness to God in whatever dealings you take up. Be honest and truthful in all your business dealings. Consider yourself to be an instrument of God. Hence, keep aside a portion of your income for spending on the poor and the needy. The Lord will accept all that you do as an offering. Consider God as your Master. Express your gratitude for His blessings by saying, 'O God! The success of my business is due to Your kindness. I am merely an agent taking care of it.' Avoid the temptation of earning easy money. This would be a good way to start your *sadhana* as a businessman."

My friend was surprised. "Do you mean to say that is all God wants from me? I was under the impression that you would prescribe some tough routines for me. Are you sure this path you recommend will take me towards God? It sounds too simple to be true."

I smiled and said to him, "It may sound simple; but it requires good intention, firm determination and a heart that is pure and detached. If you are able to carry out these disciplines, you will indeed be richly blessed."

I would recommend the same to any of you, who, like my friend, are committed to your family as well as your business or profession. In fact, I often tell my friends that it is far easier for a householder to fulfil his *swadharma*, for he has his work cut out for him. But let me also add a note of caution; this attitude to life and work and family, is not easy to cultivate. To be able to function in this prudent way you need to do some *sadhana*.

Here are the words of Sage Lao Tse:

> Continuing to fill a pail after
> it is full, water will be wasted.
> Continuing to grind an axe after it
> is sharp will wear it away.
>
> Excess of light blinds the eye!
> Excess of sound deafens the ear!
> Excess of sweets deadens the taste!
>
> He who possesses moderation is
> lasting and enduring.
> Too much is always a curse.
> Most of all in wealth.

May I say to you, moderation is in itself a tremendous *sadhana* that we must all learn to practise. The ancients called it the 'golden mean' – this attempt to choose the middle path between extremes.

Let me make my standpoint clear. Money is not all evil. Acquiring wealth is not a sin.

A friend once said to me somewhat accusingly, "Dada, I appreciate your concern for the downtrodden and deprived. But, is there no room in your heart for those whom God has chosen to bless with wealth? Is it wrong to be wealthy?"

I couldn't help smiling at this unexpected question. "No, my dear friend," I replied, "it is certainly *not* a sin to be wealthy. I believe, it is one's good *karma* that makes one wealthy in this life. And in my heart, there is profound gratitude for all those wealthy brothers and sisters who support the various activities of the Sadhu Vaswani Mission and other similar organisations. Whatever made you think that I love them any less than the people whom they help us to serve?"

I have nothing against money – and I have nothing but respect for wealthy people who have earned their money through hard work and righteous means. There is nothing wrong with earning money. There is nothing wrong in investing your money wisely for the security of your loved ones. All I say to my friends is – do not become obsessed with making money. Do not labour under the impression that money is the be-all and end-all of life. Do not equate material possessions with happiness. Do not equate your 'success' with possessions.

To put in another way – of course it is good to have all the luxuries that money can buy; all I say to you is that you must not miss out on all the wonderful things that money *cannot* buy!

The preacher Billy Graham once remarked: "There is nothing wrong with men possessing riches. The wrong comes when riches possess men." This, in effect, is the success of moderation! *You* must possess your riches; they must not possess you!

Here is a question that people often ask me: "Is it wrong to aspire for wealth? Are material wealth and worldly happiness an impediment on the path of spirituality?"

My answer is this: when you begin to tread the path of spiritual awareness, then you will find that you do not really aspire for material possessions. You leave it to the Lord.

It is for God to give you whatever He likes. God is our Master – and let me assure you, He is a very benevolent Master! This awareness helps you to surrender the thread of your life in His safe, benevolent hands – and you will find miracles happening in your daily life.

Let me add, people choose different paths in their lives. Some of them are engrossed in worldly affairs. They think money; they dream money; they live and work for money. Yet others are there, totally immersed in the life of the Spirit. To them, the outer world and its many manifestations is all *maya* – illusion.

"Why is this so?" a friend once asked me. "Why is it that God gives the wealth of the world to some people, and the wealth of the spirit to others? Does He not want all of us to realise Him and reach Him?"

I smiled and said to him, "This is like asking the Headmaster of a school, 'Why are there twelve different grades/classes in your school? Why is it that some children are in the first standard and others are in the tenth standard? Don't you want all your students to pass the highest examination?"

"Yes, the Headmaster would certainly like all his students to pass the highest examination, eventually. But in order to do that, they have to go through the different stages of education."

Likewise, God wants each and everyone of us to realise Him and reach Him. But we have to pass through different stages to attain Him. Many of us are engrossed in worldly affairs. Surely, a time will come when the things of this world can no longer satisfy us. Then, we will have to turn inward, Godward.

To those of you engaged in business, commerce and the

professions, let me say to you: these pursuits are not incompatible with spirituality! There is no need for us to give up our worldly duties and obligations in order to seek spiritual fulfilment. But we must learn, in the midst of our hectic schedules and business activities, to withdraw ourselves from the world for a while and give ourselves wholly to God. Then we must return to our daily work, pouring into it the energy of the Spirit. Such work will bless the world. Through such work will God, Himself, descend upon the earth. Work of the true type is a bridge between God and humanity. So, with one hand let us cling to His Lotus Feet and with the other, attend to our daily duties. Believe me, it is not as difficult as you think! As a self-discipline, it becomes second nature with practice.

Many people claim to be pious, good, devoted and absolutely committed to their family, their community and their faith. But, when it comes to their business interests, they find nothing wrong in claiming that they have to be "ruthless" in order to survive and prosper. "It's a cut-throat world," they claim. "If we do not indulge in such practices we will not be in business!"

Yet others compromise on product quality – shoddy workmanship, poor safety standards and cheap components. Their 'justification' is this – "We are not here for charity; we are in business."

They say India loses billions of rupees every year through tax evasion – yet another dishonest practice that businessmen consider to be their prerogative.

Swiss banks were, at one time, equated with the security and confidentiality of the highest order. Now, we associate them with corrupt practices, illegally amassed wealth and 'black' money.

Do not think that I blame businessmen alone for dishonesty with money. The truth is, many of us fall a victim to dishonesty when it comes to money. This is why I urge everyone to develop the right attitude to money, money-making and wealth.

How many of us give our 100% to our jobs? An executive once said to me, "In any organisation Dada, you will find 90% of the work done by 10% of the people. The rest just don't do their best."

Honesty to your work, honesty to your employer is as important for salaried people just as honesty in cash dealings is important for businessmen. We have to *earn* our salary – every rupee of it.

Public servants are in the 'exalted' position where they can genuinely help and serve large masses of people. But, how many of them abuse their position and power to accept, nay, *demand* bribes to do what is their duty, the job that they are actually paid to do?

Corruption is a two-sided weapon. For everyone who receives a bribe, someone must be there who *gives* a bribe. When people offer money to get their work done fast, to bend the rule or even break the law, that is also dishonesty.

Professionals like lawyers and doctors need to be scrupulously honest with their clients/patients. Such professions depend on integrity and trust and it is indeed a sad state of affairs when such people are tainted by dishonest practices.

'Honesty', therefore, has several dimensions. It is a complete moral code by which we live our lives. I cannot be honest with my family, but dishonest at work; I cannot claim to be truly honest, if I am true to my friends but untrue to my clients and customers; I cannot claim to be 'good' if I donate millions in charity but 'cook up' accounts to make illegal profits. Indeed, honesty and integrity are the basic *sadhanas* that every businessman and professional should cultivate.

Honesty is not a separate, exclusive moral code reserved only for one part of your life, one segment of your conscience. It is a way of right living, right action, right speech and right thinking. What we all need is honesty in life, in thought, action and words. You cannot 'practise' honesty for one or two hours a day, for it is not a ritual reserved for partial adoption; it is, as I said, a way of life.

I believe that honesty is so critically linked with money matters because money management is one of the greatest lessons we must learn in the school of life. Honesty in money matters is the ultimate lesson, because it enables us to realise that money is not the be-all and end-all of life. Honesty in money matters enables us to strive towards detachment, which is one of the supreme virtues. When a man distances himself from money, when he overcomes greed, which is nothing but excessive desire for money, he has truly become an evolved being. He then comes to realise that the wealth of this world is, in Sadhu Vaswani's words, a *loan* that is given to mankind to be spent in the service of all. He knows that if he has 'made' money successfully, it is a blessing that he must share with those less fortunate than himself.

Money, wealth, prosperity, thus becomes the ultimate test of honesty to oneself. If you or I can ask ourselves: "Am I slave to my money, or am I truly the *master* of my money?" – if we can ask and answer that question in all honesty, we will all come to realise what our Honesty Quotient is!

Here are a few suggestions that the businessman/professional who aspires to a life of *sadhana* can put into practise:

- Respect wealth, treat your money with care and reverence. But know that the worst form of disrespect to money – and therefore, irreverence to *Lakshmi* – is to earn it by lying, cheating or falsehood. Therefore, cultivate the discipline of Right Livelihood; ensure that your wealth is acquired by fair and honest means without harming anyone else. Right Livelihood is the basic *sadhana* for all businessmen and professionals.

- Be aware that money is *not* meant to be hoarded, stashed away, locked up in vaults and safes. Money is for *spending* – and the more we spend it on doing good for ourselves and others, to make ourselves and others happy, the more we will realise the sense of true prosperity! This is the *sadhana* of *seva* or selfless service; I believe he is dear to Him who is the support of the poor and the weak – for He is known as *Deenabandhu* and *Deenanath*.

- Always cherish the still, small voice of the conscience within you. It is a soft, inner voice which is likely to be drowned in the shout and clamour of the big, bad world. It is up to us to ensure that it is always kept alert, alive and sharp. Do not allow the voice of your conscience to be extinguished – for it is your guide to right thinking and right living. Therefore, spend a little time in silence everyday.

- Respect yourself. When you hold yourself in high esteem, you will never stoop to dishonesty and falsehood. You will never allow yourself to feel ashamed of your actions. You will be able to sleep peacefully, face your family and friends with a clear conscience, and keep your daily appointment with God in an upward-looking, aspirational mood.

- Take care of the company you keep. Let your friends be those who are aware that to respect money (to worship *Lakshmi*) is to spend it in meaningful ways.

- Make God your partner. Change your outlook. Do not merely depend on your own efforts, your own endeavours. Keep your ego out – and let God enter your life. Learn to act as His agent. Therefore, help others. You will never feel the lack – for it is He who provides, and His coffers are ever full.

- Share what you have with others. Set apart a portion of your wealth to be utilised in the service of God's suffering children. This is what we call in the Sindhi language, *barkat*.

- If a needy friend, relative or stranger calls on you urgently for financial aid, realise that the call is not made upon you, but upon God. He is the inexhaustible source of life and all the bounties of life. All you need to do is become His instrument, His channel through which His help may flow to those in need.

- Do not for a moment think that it is you who gives. The giver is God Himself. Our resources are limited; His are inexhaustible and infinite. Contact God, again and again. Stay connected to His abundance.

- Let this prayer be upon your lips: "God, make me a channel of Your Mercy!" And to become a channel of His Mercy, surrender all you are and all you have at His Lotus Feet.

Exercise in Ethical Business Decisions

Kirk O. Hanson, in his book *Good Start*, suggests certain simple questions that the entrepreneur must ask himself, before he makes key decisions:

a) Who will be helped by this decision?

b) Who will be harmed by this decision?

c) Am I taking the risk of violating anyone's rights, or of breaking promises that I made, or undermining the trust reposed in me by following this course of action?

d) Are there other/better alternatives that are consistent with my commitments and obligations, and which would produce a greater balance of good over harm or no harm at all?

At first, this exercise may seem time-consuming and difficult. But as you habitually learn to examine each decision ethically, it will become a spontaneous exercise.

Five Steps On The Path For Businessmen

1. Greet difficulties with a smile and meet dangers with love. Never forget that the Lord Divine is ever with you – protecting you, guiding you, guarding you. In times of crisis, you will feel the *thrill of protection*. Whisper to yourself, "The Mother is holding me by the hand: I feel safe and secure." The Mother never fails. Let us not fail Her. Trust in Her till the breaking point, and the breaking point will never come.

2. Let prayer become a habit with you. Pray, pray and continue to pray. So many of our prayers remain unanswered because we give up praying. We become impatient and lose faith. We feel that as God is not going to act for us, we must act for ourselves. We forget that God acts at the appointed time. If He has not yet acted, it only means that the right time is not yet. This applies not only to material requirements but also, to mental and spiritual needs.

3. Pray for more and more faith. He who has faith has everything. For, verily, "faith moves mountains". Pray for faith as a famished person prays for food and a thirsty person for water. What is it to have faith? It is to feel sure that whatever God does is always for the best. It is to grow in the realisation that when God denies His child some good, He designs to give him something better.

4. The cure of all ills – physical, mental, spiritual – is contact with God. From time to time, detach yourself from your surroundings and enter within the depth of your

soul. In silence wait upon God, conscious of His presence. From time to time, engage yourself in loving conversation with God. Offer all your work to Him: pray to Him for help and blessing, before beginning any work: and express your gratitude to Him when it is over.

5. Accept whatever comes to you. Do not seek the 'pleasant': do not shun the 'unpleasant'. Rejoice in everything that happens. All that has happened, all that is happening and is yet to happen – is for the best! Turn away all thoughts of fear and doubt and anxiety. Close the windows and doors of your minds against them as you would against plague germs. Face each trial and tribulation with love and laughter. Meet every situation in life with the prayer of St Francis de Sales – the prayer of which I am never tired, the prayer which is an effective formula for inner peace, "Yes, Father! Yes, and always yes!"

Ask Yourself

- Do I feel a sense of emptiness or loneliness within me in spite of everything I have?

- What do wealth, power, possessions, name, fame mean to me?

- Do I earn my money honestly and truthfully?

- Do I thank God for the abundant gifts He has given me?

- Am I attached to my possessions?

- Do I share my wealth with those in need?

- Do I feel money can get me everything in life?

- Do I listen to my conscience?

Sadhana for the *Grihasta* or Householder

The Hindu scriptures refer to the married state as *Grihasta Ashrama*. May I draw your attention to the use of the word *ashrama* here; the *ashrama* is a place or a state that denotes discipline and restraint. Thus, marriage according to the Hindu ideals is not a pleasure hunting ground. It is not a licence to do as one pleases. It is at once a discipline and a responsibility. In marriage, two persons – a man and a woman – offer the whole of their self, mind, body and feelings to each other. They cease to live for their selfish ends; they live for each other, for their families and for the promotion and propagation of *dharma* or righteousness. True marriage thus becomes an *abhyasa* to attain to God.

Hindu *shastras* emphasise the value of *grihasta ashrama* as fundamental to the well-being of society. This is because the people in the other three *ashramas* (i.e. *brahmacharya* or bachelor state, *vanaprastha* or retired/contemplative state and *sanyasa* or the state of the renunciate) depend on the *grihasta* (householder) for sustenance and support. They need the *grihasta's* help to carry out their duties. As for the *grihasta*, he is permitted to earn his living by the right means in order to support his family, raise his children and perform those acts of charity and compassion that assist others in the three *ashramas*.

I often tell my married friends that they are lucky to be in the *grihasta ashrama,* where all they have to do is perform their duty well in order to attain salvation. However, this is not as easy as it sounds!

Saints and sages refer to the life of the *grihasta* as *jivayagna* – a life-long saga of service and sacrifice for family and society. Is this not a *sadhana* in itself?

Another Sanskrit term for marriage is *vivaha,* which literally means "what supports or carries". The *vivaha* ceremony thus creates a union which supports and sustains a man and woman throughout their married life in the pursuit of *dharma* (righteousness.)

Of the sixteen *samskaras* (sacraments) associated with Hinduism, *vivaha* or marriage is considered to be the most sacred, for the *grihasta ashrama* is considered to be the basis of all the other *ashramas.* Therefore, Hindu scriptures eulogise *vivaha* in glowing terms.

Marriage is not meant to satisfy carnal desires. Rather, it is meant to assist one's spiritual progress, leading to God-realisation through a disciplined life. In marriage, a young man and woman practise self-discipline and self-control, even as they find support and companionship with the spouse and other members of the family, and learn to offer selfless service to society.

Marriage may be said to be a co-operative venture between husband and wife in the field of the four *purusharthas* – *dharma, artha, kama,* and *moksha.* It is the union of two souls, and this sacred union is formalised through sacrament.

Vivaha is also literally translated to mean upliftment. Marriage helps young couples to raise themselves towards God. The bond of marriage unites two souls so firmly that though they are physically two separate entities, their souls are merged into one harmonious whole. Together, they vow always to:

• Have faith in the Divine.

- Show love, devotion and compassion to one another.

- Help in each other's good deeds.

- Strive to keep their minds pure and virtuous.

- Be strong and righteous.

- Show respect and affection to each other's parents and families.

- Raise their children to be strong in body and mind and pure in spirit.

- Welcome guests to their home.

It is significant that in one of the rituals that form part of the Hindu marriage called *laja homa* (prayer for shared prosperity), husband and wife take turns to lead one another around the fire, signifying that both are capable of leadership and guidance.

In the *Gospel of Sri Ramakrishna* there are several sections entitled 'Advice to Householders'. This just goes to show the great importance that Sri Ramakrishna Paramahansa attached to marriage and home. When we speak about the *grihasta ashrama*, let us not forget that we are talking about over 90% of the adult population who belong to this category. We find Sri Ramakrishna passing on valuable advice to his devotees about the duties of a *grihasta*.

In those days – perhaps even now – these people tended to undervalue themselves. Many of them would tell Sri Ramakrishna, "After all, we are only *grihastas*: What can we achieve?" or "We are only *grihastas*: how can we hope to attain God?"

The Saint's answer to them was simple: "Why can you not attain God? He is the *Antaryami* – the Inner Ruler who is within each one of us. Think of Him constantly in your daily life as you do your work. You will find that He will take care of you!"

The *grihasta* is one who lives in a *griha* or home. The first thing he must realise is that this home is not a prison. It is a household.

When does a home become a prison – you may ask. It becomes a veritable prison when the people living in it restrict their lives, confining their minds to *I* and *Mine*. "Get rid of *I* and *Mine*," Sri Ramakrishna told the *grihastas* repeatedly. When we are trapped in this narrow circle of egoism and selfishness, we lose the sense of the vastness and magnificence of the universe of which we are a part. We lose the sense of dignity and responsibility that is attached to the great *grishasta ashrama*.

To be a true *grihasta* one must cherish the institution of marriage and one must develop self-confidence and self-reliance. One must stop constantly devaluing oneself by saying, "I am only a *grihasta*. I am only a *samsari* – I am tied down by my bonds."

No! Cast aside such doubts, strengthen your mind, broaden your vision and vow to contribute to the betterment of your culture, your community, your society, your country and the world you live in. This is your prerogative as a *grihasta*, a true citizen.

How may we shed the feeling of regret, of confinement associated with being a *grihasta*? Here again, Sri Ramakrishna has the answer – Live in *samsara* (the world), but don't allow *samsara* (worldliness) to live in you. He gives us the example of the boat and urges that the boat must be on the waters – but the water must not be allowed to enter the boat else the boat will sink and we all will be drowned. The new *grihastas* of the new millennium can learn from the Saint of Dakshineshwar how to make their married life glorious – by working together as enlightened citizens in a spirit of love and service.

I am deeply saddened when I hear a woman say, "I am only a housewife." What she expresses in these words is the regret that she is not a working woman, not a professional, but someone confined to the four walls of the home. She does not know her real dignity and worth. If only she realises her onerous duties and responsibilities as a builder of the home, as the shaper of a new generation, as the architect of a new India, she would not refer to herself in such belittling terms.

Sadhana for *Grihastas:*

1. Grow together spiritually – this is my advice to all young married couples. 'Individuals' will collide if they are in conflict with other 'individuals'. But well-rounded, well-developed 'personalities' do not clash. Sri Ramakrishna distinguished between unripe and ripe mangoes – between unripe individuals who are unable to escape the narrow confines of the 'I' and 'Mine' and those that have evolved spiritually and become truly human. If husband and wife remain unripe, the home will be reduced to a site of conflict and tension. When they become ripe the home will be a temple of peace and harmony.

2. Learn to respect, cherish and promote each other's spiritual aspirations. Do not stand in the way, do not be intolerant or insensitive to such inclinations in your partner.

3. As we saw, the Vedas have outlined a fourfold purpose for human life – *dharma, artha, kama* and *moksha.* In an ideal marriage, the couple's life must be rooted in *dharma* – ethical values. Without compromising these values, they should establish meaningful human relationships (*kama*) and secure their financial assets (*artha*). This should be utilised to promote *dharma* and move towards the ultimate goal of *moksha* (liberation). I do believe that the ideal marriage is one in which the two partners actively help each other attain this goal.

It was a wise philospher who said, "Life is like a house. Without *dharma*, the house has no foundation. Without *artha*, it has no walls. Without *kama*, it has no furnishings. Without *moksha*, it has no roof."

4. Do not separate your *sadhana* or spiritual efforts from the daily activities of your married life. Do not separate your worldly and spiritual activities in exclusive compartments. Rather, learn to perform your duty, carry out your responsibilities to the family

in the spirit of *karma yoga*, as suggested by the Gita. In other words, make of your married life, an offering to the Lord Himself. Whatever it is you may be doing – teaching a child, helping him with his homework, attending to household chores, balancing the budget or attending to guests – let it be done as an act of worship to God, in the spirit of fulfilling your *swadharma* (the duty allotted to you). In this way, marriage does not remain a worldly attachment which ties you down; it becomes a *sadhana* which helps you evolve.

5. Realise that every situation, every predicament you face in your marriage is helping you to achieve your goal of self-realisation. When your partner displeases you, you grow in the virtue of patience. When you encounter disappointments, you imbibe the spirit of acceptance. When an offense is committed against you, you grow in the spirit of forgiveness.

6. Make a pact with each other from Day 1: that the two of you will never ever lose your temper at the same time. Should you happen to quarrel with each other during the day, don't let the sun set on your quarrel – in other words, make up with each other before the day is over. Should you happen to quarrel at night, don't let the sun rise on your quarrel.

It is also a healthy practice never to lose your temper at the same time with your child. The child cannot cope with the combined displeasure and anger of both his parents berating him or scolding him for any wrong he may have committed. The mother must adopt a conciliatory attitude when the father is disciplining the child and the father must take on this role when the mother pulls up the child. This way, the child is assured that he has one parent at least on his side, in a moment of crisis.

7. Planning the family budget is both a *sadhana* in economics as well as a *sadhana* in selfless spending! Husband and wife must cooperate with each other to see that the family expenditure is kept within reasonable limits and does not exceed the income. In

these days of plastic money and credit card loans, restraint and prudence must govern all individual spending so that the family savings and investments for a rainy day are intact, and a reasonable amount of income is reserved for your favourite charity.

In this connection, I would like to share an amusing anecdote with you. A young married woman went out shopping to her favourite boutique, and was completely captivated by a beautiful dress that she saw on display. The price was astronomical! But she felt she had to buy it, because it was so gorgeous, and it would make her look divine.

But the price caused a serious qualm, and to overcome the obstacle immediately, she called up her husband on the cellphone. The husband, who was attending an important meeting with a potential client, came on line, and she said to him, "Oh darling! There is this absolutely gorgeous dress that I have seen at the boutique today. Can I buy it please?"

The husband was smart. He knew all the right questions to be asked at such a juncture. "What's the price?" he demanded to be told. The wife quoted the price, and he overcame a momentary fainting sensation by holding on to the chair firmly.

After a moment's pause, he said to his wife, "Honey, you know we can't afford to spend that kind of money now."

"But I have my credit card with me," said the wife. "You can settle the bill next month."

"You know fully well that we have other important bills pending on the card," said the husband patiently. "You are intelligent honey, and you must not give in to such needless extravagances."

"But you don't know how beautiful I will look in this dress," the wife persisted. "Whatever you say darling, I am seriously tempted to buy it."

"Honey, temptation is Satan's old trick! Don't fall for it. Say to him firmly, 'Get thee behind me, Satan,' and put the dress away."

"Honey, are you there?" he asked anxiously after a long period of silence from her end.

"I said, 'Get thee behind me, Satan' the wife reported dutifully, 'but he says, 'Lady, you look simply splendid from behind.'"

8. Always show the greatest possible respect to the elders on both sides of the family. Remember, you are not only doing your duty to your parents and elders, but also setting an example for your children to follow.

Mr. Joshi had decided that his elderly father was to be sent to a senior citizens' Home. Heedless to the protests of the old man, he filled forms, paid the necessary amount, and dropped the old man at the Home.

A week later, he had a phone call from the Home asking him to bring a blanket for his father. This article had been left out from the list given to him by the Home. Mr. and Mrs. Joshi turned out their linen cupboard and picked up an old blanket which they felt was pretty useless to them. Mr. Joshi wrapped the blanket in an old newspaper and set out for the Home.

"It's a big blanket Papa," said his teenage son Rahul. "Why don't you cut it up and give grandfather one half? It would be more than enough for him, he is so frail."

"But what would we do with the other half, Rahul?"

"Well, we could keep it safely, and it will come in useful when *I* put *you* in the Senior Citizen's Home, would it not?"

There was a moment of stunned silence – and wisdom began to dawn on Mr. Joshi.

Most married men are fully aware of their duty, their obligation and their responsibility to their wives. I only urge them to remember that care and concern for your wife should not translate itself into neglect of your parents and elders.

9. Realise that your children are your greatest responsibility.

They are not toys for you to play with; they are not your future insurance. They are souls whom the Lord has entrusted in your care. Do not pamper or indulge them mindlessly. Blend firmness with affection, discipline with love, to give them a secure and healthy environment where they might grow to absorb the deeper values of life.

Here is a prayer I read somewhere:

Let there be harmony between husband and wife.
Let there be harmony between parents and their children.
Let there be harmony among different relatives.
Let there be harmony among friends.
Let there be harmony among the elements.
Let there be harmony between the earth and the sky.
Let harmony be experienced everywhere.
May God bless you with harmony and peace.

I urge all my friends: if you want to build a happy home and family, make God the centre of your home. I am afraid many of us today have thrown God out of our homes. This has created a vacuum – and when there is a vacuum created in life, the devil rushes in to fill it.

Bring God back into your home, so that the devil can have no place there. One way to do this is for the family to spend some time together daily, in God's presence. All the members of the family from the oldest to the youngest must get together for at least 15 minutes in God's presence, and hold a brief 'prayer meeting'. You can sing the Lord's Name, chant your favourite *mantra*, do a little *kirtan* or have a reading from the scriptures or from the words of your guru. You can pick up a thought for the day from a great thinker and each of you can say what you feel about it.

God is the source of all that is good in life. He is the source of understanding, tolerance, insight, patience and love. It is easy to acquire these virtues when you put yourself in His hands. When you pray together, you restore peace, balance and harmony to your marriage and family. When you take a disagreement or misunderstanding to God, you remove it from the realm of human bitterness.

When the spiritual element enters marriage, when the presence of God is asserted in the marriage, then that marriage is truly made in heaven. It becomes the supreme highway on which two linked souls walk towards one ultimate goal. They are linked to each other through golden chains of love, understanding and devotion.

"The family," said the Blessed Mother Teresa, "is the place to learn God. God created the family – together as husband, wife and children – to reflect His love."

PEACE AND CONTENTMENT IN MARRIAGE

A man lived in a small cottage with his wife and five children. He was greatly devoted to his guru, and had received a guru *mantra* for peace and contentment from his master. However, the man was deeply frustrated with his lot; he longed for a better environment, better living conditions in the home. Feeling rather let down, he complained to his guru: "I cannot even recite my guru *mantra* in peace. Please help me; make my life a little easier."

The guru said to him, "I will give you certain instructions; if you follow them carefully, things will improve miraculously. But you must do exactly as I say for a month."

The man agreed to follow the guru's instructions in letter and spirit. Forthwith, the guru asked him to take a cow into the cottage and care for it. He had to feed it, wash it and groom it everyday and clean its vicinity. The man was asked to return after ten days.

Being an obedient disciple, the man followed the guru's advice; he returned after ten days, quite weary with the added burden of looking after the cow. Now, the guru sent a dog with him, asking him to take care of the animal. The constant mooing and barking in the house, not to mention the demands made by the animals on his time and effort, had frayed the man's nerves quite thin. But he obeyed the guru implicitly, returning to report his progress after ten days.

This time, the guru gave him a chattering monkey and entrusted its upkeep to him. Now there were seven people and three animals in the cottage, all living under the same roof.

The man returned to pay his respects to the guru at the end of the month. Caring for the animals had taken its toll on him, and he was quite exhausted. But such was his longing for peace and contentment that he did not utter a word of complaint. Such was his faith in the guru.

This time, the guru gave him a new instruction. "Release all the animals and return to your old routine," he told the man. "Come and see me after a week."

The man returned at the end of a week. "How is your home now?" enquired the guru. "Master, it is like heaven on earth," the man replied, elated. "I am at peace now and content with my life."

Comforts and luxuries cannot bring us peace. Contentment is the secret of harmony in the home.

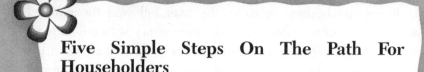

Five Simple Steps On The Path For Householders

1. Perhaps, the simplest and most efficacious method of *sadhana* that the family can practise together is that of *kirtan*. Whenever two or three gather together, let them sing in chorus the Name of the Divine Lord and in the Name lose themselves. This method is so simple that often its importance is overlooked. But it is one of immense value to us all. Get together with your family, friends and neighbours and form *kirtan* bands. You will sanctify your own lives: you will purify, as did Sri Chaitanya centuries ago, the atmosphere of your town and country: you will release forces for the healing of the human race.

2. As you wake up in the morning, breathe out an aspiration of purity, love, peace, humility, trust – any aspiration that may express your inmost need. Repeat this aspiration as often as you can during the day, even in the midst of your work.

3. As you retire at night, read a little from the life or teachings of a saint, a *bhakta*, a man of God as this has a purifying influence on the mind and, consequently, on one's dream-consciousness. I have found the following books specially useful – *The Imitation of Christ* by Thomas Á Kempis; *The Gospel of Sri Ramakrishna* by "M" and Sadhu Vaswani's *Gita Meditations, Master and Mystics* and *The Rishi*; *God Calling* by Two Listeners; *Readings from Sufi Mystics*; *Selections from Meister Eckhart*; *Practice of the*

Presence of God by Brother Lawrence – the list is endless.

4. When evil thoughts come to you, do not struggle with them. The more you struggle, the more you strengthen them. The best way to fight evil thoughts is to let them alone and to think on divine thoughts. Light dispels darkness. Every good thought is like a ray of light which dispels the dark clouds of evil thoughts.

5. Keep yourself relaxed at all times – both in body and in mind. So, work with unhastened speed: and speak gently, sweetly, in love and understanding. And let nothing disturb your inner peace. Imagine the world as an ocean with stormy waves rising high, threatening to drown you: be still and full of trust in the Lord of the ocean. The waves will pass away.

Practical Exercises for Couples:

Here are a few questions that couples can ask themselves to ensure that they are working to make their marriage successful as well as meaningful:

1. Am I forgiving by nature?

When you refuse to forgive your spouse, you are building barriers in your marriage. Molehills become mountains and trivial issues snowball into major controversies.

2. How often do you say "I'm sorry" to your spouse?

Being able to take responsibility for your actions and learning to admit mistakes is a very important step on the spiritual path. This is an exercise which must begin at home.

3. How often do you appreciate your spouse?

In marriage, as in life, this is the secret of happiness: stop complaining, start appreciating.

4. How often do you put your spouse's interest first?

Selfishness can never bring us true joy. Putting others first is an invaluable exercise in true happiness.

5. Do you consult your spouse in all the major decisions you take?

Mutual respect and mutual understanding are fostered when 'I' is replaced by 'we' in all decisions.

6. How often do you pray together?

Some couples may be surprised by this question, but this is an exercise which does wonders for your marriage.

Ask Yourself

- Do I consider living a married life as my spiritual path to reaching God?

- In the midst of my daily work, do I remember God?

- Do I fight with my family or do I let go off my ego and remain detached?

- While serving my family, do I offer my services to God?

- Do I cherish the institution of marriage every day?

- Do I separate my *sadhana* or spiritual efforts from the daily activities of my married life?

- Do I treat my daily household chores as a worship to God?

- Do I realize that my greatest responsibility is my children?

- How often do I pray together with my family?

Sadhana for Beginners

I believe every one of us realises at one stage or another that life on this earth is transient and that the journey of the soul must continue even after we have ceased to be here. Even those of us who refuse to acknowledge God and dismiss the concept of the soul are mystified and intrigued by what awaits us after death. In short, everyone agrees that a new chapter begins at the point of death.

For those of us who follow the Hindu way of life, our perception is very clear: the purpose of this human life is to escape from the wheel of birth, death and rebirth and attain Union with God: this Union in Hindu terminology is therefore called as true Liberation, *Mukti*, which is above and beyond all worldly notions of freedom.

As firm believers in the Law of *Karma* which I like to describe as The Law of the Seed, we Hindus subscribe to the very scientific and yet profoundly Hindu belief: as we sow, so shall we reap. Each one of us has been given a plot – the field of our life. In this field of life, we are sowing seeds everyday. Every thought I think, every word I utter, every deed I perform, every emotion that I arouse within my heart, every feeling, every fancy, every wish – all these are seeds I am sowing in the field of my life. There are also the seeds we have sown in our past existence, which we are reaping now. The present is thus the effect of the past. Therefore, it follows logically, that the past and the present together will determine the future. Thus, *karma* is not a destiny which we cannot escape. Rather, we are the architects of our own destiny – for, by accumulating good *karma*, thinking good thoughts, cultivating good feelings, speaking good words and performing good actions – we can actually change our future.

Is this not *sadhana* at its best? It is the *sadhana* of daily life, living life as it ought to be lived.

The second most important law of Hinduism, I shall call the Law of the Wheel.

There are some questions that have always troubled seekers on the path: Why is there so much suffering in this world? Why is it that even good people suffer? Why does God allow evil and injustice which we see wherever we turn? What happens to us when we die?

The Law of the Wheel, which is the law of rebirth or reincarnation, emphasises another cardinal Hindu doctrine: the body dies; but the soul does not die. Is this not the great truth that Lord Krishna asserts to Arjuna in the Bhagavad Gita?

> The *atman* is not born, nor can it ever die. It never came into being, nor ceaseth to be! Birthless, deathless, changeless still, abiding and ancient is the *atman*! It is not slain, even though the body is slain! [II – 20]

The *Chandogya Upanishad* too, expresses the same truth: "Verily, indeed, when Life hath left it, this body dies. But the Life does not die."

The body is a garment worn by man as long as he needs it; it is cast off when it is old and worn out; the soul then wears another garment. The garment, the body, is *not* the self. The body dies, but the soul does not. The soul bears with it the impressions, the essence of its experiences in this earthly life.

Each birth into which the soul enters here upon earth, is but a step in its evolution to perfection. Until this goal of perfection is reached, the soul enters another body, assumes another earthly existence and is re-born. The cycle of birth and death is repeated until the goal of perfection is ultimately attained.

This, then, is the goal of life. The goal we hope to attain through *sadhana:* The goal of Perfection and Union with the Source of all life, the Supreme Being, which, for want of a better word, we call God.

The journey to this desired destination begins with awareness: that we are pilgrims upon the path of life. And while we are treading this path, it is very important that we are not distracted by the pursuit of shadow-shapes that come and go. For what are wealth, power, authority, position, name and fame, but shadow shapes that come and go? Name and fame are won and lost even as fortunes are built and lost on the stock exchange; youth and beauty are like the fleeting rainbow which appears out of nowhere and disappears into nothingness, leaving not a trace behind.

This path of life is therefore called the path of self-realisation. It is a difficult path, "sharp as the edge of a razor" to quote the *Upanishads*. And one must tread this path, step by step.

For the beginner on the path, the very first step is awakening: we awaken to this truth that the "self" or *atman* is distinct from the body, the *stula sharira* or physical vehicle which it inhabits.

Awakening comes in a variety of ways. But it is always a gift of grace.

With awakening comes the realisation that the body is a Temple of God. It must not be soiled; it must be kept clean and pure, so that it might become a channel of God's forces in this world of darkness and death.

Let me hasten to add: the body must not be neglected. For it is like a musical instrument which is given to each one of us, to participate in the harmony that is life. If you give a musician a broken instrument, he can only produce harsh, discordant notes on it. So too, if you desire to produce the beautiful melody of the spirit, the instrument of your body must be fit and sound and pure from internal blemish. Therefore, the claims of the body must not be ignored.

The second step is control over the senses, the mind and the lower passions.

A well-established doctor once confided in me that very often, when a pretty female patient came for consultation, he would get disturbed and become subject to impure desires. He had a beautiful wife and was a great doctor. But, unfortunately, he had little control over his mind which gave rise to vicious desires of lust.

It is strange that we may have mastered knowledge gained from books; we may have read scriptures; but all the knowledge and reading does not give us the wisdom and the strength to control our minds. Hence, a trifling incident or experience arouses undesirable thoughts and emotions within us. This happens because our hearts are impure. It is said that what is in your heart is mirrored in your life. A true human being is one who is blessed with a pure heart. A man who has a pure heart knows that in this universe we are all connected, we are all interdependent.

Greater, infinitely greater, than brain power is the power of the will. This is what we need to succeed in life. Very often we procrastinate; we keep postponing doing certain things that are essential for our spiritual growth; and this is because of our weak will power. We need will power and will power can be bestowed on us by the Guru. It is in the company of the Guru that we become large-hearted. We become devoted; we learn to purify our hearts.

May I tell you, the man who lacks will power and has an impure heart is no better than an animal. He may be rich in the wealth of this world, he may have position and power which impresses the world: but all this counts for nothing on the spiritual path.

We must strive to rise above the animalistic tendencies. We must strive to be good human beings. We must live this life of ours with a strong will power and a large and pure heart.

The third step is the practice of silence.

The practice of silence is not child's play. It is a tough and demanding discipline. Many of you who have attempted to meditate can vouch for this – the moment we sit in silence to meditate, our mind begins to wander, because the nature of the mind is to wander. It is not only in this birth alone that the mind wanders; it has been wandering through so many births that we have lived earlier. We are born with this restless and roaming mind. That is why, the moment we sit in silence to meditate, all the suppressed thoughts wake up and the mind seems to go berserk, struggling like a frail ship against a rough turbulent sea.

In the Bhagavad Gita, Arjuna asks Sri Krishna, "O, Lord, the mind is akin to a storm of lust and desires, and man is carried away by the storm. Is it possible to tame this turbulent mind?" Sri Krishna replies, "O Arjuna, it is true that the mind is like a raging storm. It is difficult to control it, but it is not impossible."

We have to transcend the mind to attain the ultimate goal of life. It is said that there are as many ways to God as there are the souls of men. There are many paths open to us, and each one can choose one's own way.

There are three paths that the Gita recommends to us:

1. *Gnana Marga* – Path of Knowledge

2. *Karma Marga* – Path of Action

3. *Bhakti Marga* – Path of Devotion

In the Bhagavad Gita, Sri Krishna describes these three *margas* and tells his dear disciple Arjuna, "Arjuna, there are three kinds of paths. And all the three paths lead to Me."

The question arises, why are there so many different paths to reach the same goal? This is because every man is made uniquely different. On the plane of manifestation, there is so much of variety, but on the plane of the Spirit, there is unity. The Spirit is one. Spirituality knows no duality.

As I said, on the plane of manifestation there is diversity, and hence, there are many paths. But they all lead to the same goal.

What is *Gnana Marga*? It is the path of true wisdom. He who walks the path of Knowledge, tries to discover the Truth. He follows the dictum, only Brahman is Truth. The world is ephemeral. Brahman is Truth. The Supreme Spirit alone is Truth. God is Truth. All else is an illusion, all else is temporary, all else will vanish and disappear. All that is manifest, which can be touched, felt and heard, is a shadow of reality, and that is why the saints and sages urge us, "O man, do not chase the shadows of the world." It is only when you become aware of the illusion, i.e. shadows, will you be able to go beyond the manifestations. Everything that is happening around us, everything that is happening to us is an illusion. The path of wisdom makes us aware that Brahman is Truth and the world is transient.

The path of knowledge is the path of self-enquiry. At every step the aspirant asks himself, 'Is this the Truth? Is this the Reality?' (For you see, this is also the path of elimination, through which we reject all that is impermanent and illusory, until we arrive at the Supreme Truth). After negating everything, the seeker arrives at the Truth, the Reality that is Brahman.

The way to arrive at the Truth is the way of negating everything. The world we live in is treacherous. It deceives us, enslaves us with its myriad manifestations. Hence, it is not easy for the common man to follow this path. Let me give you an example: while walking, if a thorn or glass piece pricks the flesh and blood oozes out, how many of us can say that the blood is not real and the pain is also not real?

Supposing you fall down and fracture a limb, you would not be able to say to yourself, "This is unreal; this is an illusion". It is very difficult to consider physical pain or hurt as an illusion and endure it in the belief that God is the only Reality.

Let me tell you, it is easy to say to others: Brahman is Truth and the world is all illusion. It is difficult to convince those suffering in pain that all their pain is physical and that all that is physical is not real. To convince others of the ultimate Reality, first I have to bear witness to it in my life. It is very difficult to prove that all around us, whatever exists is *maya*, all manifestations are illusions.

Once there lived a *jignasu*. He had chosen the *gnana marga*, the path of knowledge. As he grew older, he developed pain in the joints. The inflammation of the joints was so excruciatingly painful that he could not bear it. After suffering the pain for many days, when he was unable to endure it any longer, he at last went to see his Guru. The Guru asked him, "Where were you all these days?" The *jignasu* replied, "The pain in my joints is so acute that I could not walk." The Guru asked him, "What pain? There is no such thing as pain. For the only Reality is God, all else is an illusion." To this the *jignasu* replied, "I too have heard and believed that the only reality is God, and that all else is an illusion. The pain is an illusion. But what can I do? While the body is alive, I am unable to bear the pain. And let me tell you, dear Master, you cannot understand what I mean, because you do not have any physical illness."

Now you can see why they say that the path of Knowledge is difficult to follow.

The second path that is open to us is the path of Action (*Karma Marga*). But there is an important prerequisite, a vital condition to fulfill before we choose to follow this path: it is to first erase the ego. He who thinks that he is the doer will not be able to walk this path. An egoistic man always looks for credit but, whenever things go wrong and his actions come under scrutiny, he does not hesitate to blame God. Whenever such a person does a good job, he puffs up with pride, and gives himself the credit for all the good that is done. An egocentric man may wear a garb of humility but deep in his heart he feels elated at having accomplished the job. Hence, it is difficult to follow the path of *Karma* – which is not just action, but desireless, selfless, dedicated action.

Sri Krishna tells Arjuna, "If you want to choose the path of Action then you should learn to be gentle and humble. Think of yourself as nothing more than an instrument of God." *Nimitta matra saavya sachin.* You are but an instrument of God, Arjuna! For the energy that works through you is a part of the Supreme *shakti.* It is the power of the Divine Spirit operating through you.

Let us realise this truth: by ourselves we can do nothing. As Swami Vivekananda put it so powerfully, without God's grace, we cannot even cross the threshold of our own homes! Our 'effort' and 'ability' cannot even move a leaf.

The path of Action is also difficult. An aspirant faces many obstacles on this way. The biggest obstacle, as I said, is the ego. It is hard to be free of the egocentric self.

We are passing through *kaliyuga* – the age of evil. In this *yuga* the easiest path is *Bhakti Marga* – the path of Devotion. *Bhakti yoga* – the way of love, is the most universal and the most direct way to God. Love will discover the unity of all beings, the unity of all creation – the spiritual unity that is behind all the universe. Kindle the light of love in your heart. Surrender yourself to the Lord with utter faith. "O Lord, accept me as I am," is what the aspirant sings. *"Hari, main jaiso taiso tero."* Compared with other ways, the *Bhakti marga* appears open, spontaneous, direct and joyous. In its ecstasy, one can actually merge with God.

What this path requires is love and faith of the highest order – entreating God, surrendering oneself, seeking His forgiveness for our sins and evil deeds, beseeching His acceptance of our love, addressing Him as mother and father, pleading with Him to cleanse our minds and hearts of the accumulated filth of multiple births. This path is the path of love, for love is not an attribute of God, Love is God, and God is Love. By expanding our capacity to love we can get nearer to God. Love for the Lord should become the magnificent obsession of our lives. Awake or asleep, this love should be vibrant and make us cry out, "I love You God, I want to love You more and more. I want to love You more than anything else in the world."

In the great epic *Mahabharata,* we are told that Sri Krishna went to Hastinapur as an Ambassador of Peace. His mission was to restore cordiality and peace between the Kauravas and Pandavas. Prince Duryodhana assumed that Sri Krishna would stay with him in the royal palace. But that was not to be. Vidura's wife, who was a devotee of Lord Krishna, prayed sincerely to have Him as their guest, in their humble abode.

She called out to Him in prayer, "O Krishna! You are coming to Hastinapur, we will surely get your *darshan*, but how I wish we may offer you our loving hospitality."

Even as she prayed, she heard the voice of Sri Krishna. She went out running to see Krishna at her doorstep, and welcomed Him whole-heartedly. She did not have much by way of cooked food to offer Him, so she picked up a few bananas that they had at home, and offered them to the Lord. In her excitement and devotion, we are told, that she pealed the bananas but threw away the fruit and gave Him the banana peels to eat.

Sri Krishna savoured the banana peels, for they were offered out of true devotion. While this was happening, Vidura arrived and was shocked to see Sri Krishna eating banana peels. In utter consternation he said to his wife, "Do you realise what you are doing? You are feeding the Lord banana peels instead of the fruit."

But the true devotee that she was, his wife was oblivious to everything.

She went inside to cook food, and served it to the Lord. Sri Krishna relished the food as if it were *chappan bhog* – i.e. a delicious banquet of fifty-six varieties of delicacies. When Vidura ate the first morsel of food, he realised that his wife had forgotten to put salt in all of the dishes. He rebuked his wife, "What's wrong with you today? Why is it that you are serving Him, our Lord, saltless food and banana peels?"

Hearing this, Sri Krishna said to him, "Please do not be harsh on your wife. She has offered Me the most delicious food I have ever eaten. It is like the Divine Nectar of the Gods, because it is cooked with pure love."

The mark of true devotion – *bhakti* – is utter humility. Whenever and wherever a *bhakta* calls out to the Lord from the depth of his heart, with an intense yearning, the Lord responds without delay. He appears before the devotee, fulfilling her/his wishes.

The Lord has given us the freedom to choose the path that appeals to us, one which suits our temperament and disposition. Let us choose any path, but let us follow it sincerely. By the grace of God, one day, we shall surely reach the goal and our life will be truly blessed.

One final observation that I must make at this point, is to beginners who are overwhelmed by inadequacy and fear at the very idea of walking the path: the ways of *karma youga, jnana yoga* and *bhakti yoga* seem so exalted as to be virtually inaccessible to them. To such brothers and sisters, I offer the option of what Gurudev Sadhu Vaswani called "the little way" or the *alpa marg*!

The way of love is the "little way". It is the way of the little ones, the way which simple folk, such as we are, can tread. It is the way of *bhakti*, devotion, surrender to the Lord, by offering the love of our hearts to every creature that breathes the breath of life. It is the way of longing, deep yearning for the Soul's Beloved. As a miser longs for gold, as a lover longs for his beloved, as a child longs for its mother, even so, said Sri Ramakrishna Paramahansa, must you long for the Lord, The longing of the heart breaks forth into tears. For the little way is the way of silent, unbidden tears. And as Sant Tukaram exclaims: "Blessed are they who have tears in their eyes. The tears of *bhakti* are more precious than the holy waters of the Ganges, Jamuna and Godavari."

With tear-touched eyes, the *bhakta* cries the cry of separation: "O Lord, where art Thou? I have sought Thee, birth after birth, but have not yet been blessed with a glimpse of Thy beauteous Face. Have mercy on me, Lord, and reveal Thyself to me!"

In silence, the *bhakta* sits everyday and, in the agony of separation, cries the cry of love. Coming out of silence, as he looks around him, he finds that the world is sad, is broken, is torn with tragedy, is smitten with suffering. Such a world needs sympathy, compassion, love. And as he moves amongst men, he gives the service of love to all – the virtuous and the wicked alike. For all are the Images of the One Lord of Love: and love must be denied to none.

It is neither the will-to-power nor the will-to-live, but the will-to-become an instrument of God's help and healing, in this world of suffering and pain, that will lead to the fulfillment of man's divine destiny.

God does not demand great things of us. He wants us to walk the little way. All he asks is this: that you do your duty with devotion and dedication. God is pleased with little things, small prayers, small sacrifices, small charity, a little service; a little prayer and devotion pleases God, if it is offered in reverence and dedication.

To be drenched in love, to lose oneself in love, is to walk, in Sadhu Vaswani's meaningful words, the "little way". And to walk the little way, is to become humble as dust, is to be emptied of the 'self' and all that the 'self' stands for – the clamour and confusion of our sordid, selfish, earthly existence.

Here are a few tips for those who wish to walk the 'little way':

1. Repeat the name of God again and again. Repeat the Name Divine as you travel to work by train or bus. Keep the Name Divine in your heart as you attend to your daily work. Repeat the name as often as you can – during your evening walk, or as you gaze at the moonlit sky. Repeat the name as often as you can until the Name Divine becomes part of your breathing. Repeat the Name with love and longing.

2. Learn to engage yourself in a humble but intimate conversation with God. Entering into the silence within, speak to the Beloved! He is not from you afar! And you don't have to make elaborate preparations or notes to communicate with Him! Just trust the impulse of your heart. Tell God you need Him, you love Him and that you want to love Him more and more!

3. Let your love for God express itself in actions of love and service to those around you. Be kind and gentle to everyone who comes into contact with you. Remember that everyone who approaches you has been sent to you by God with a definite purpose.

4. Avoid saying or doing anything which will displease God. If perchance, deliberately or unknowingly, you do something wrong, seek forgiveness from those who have been hurt by your actions and from God, the all-knowing One.

5. Whatever you do, do it as an offering to God. It may be a 'lowly' act like cleaning a room or wiping the floor; or a noble deed like donating blood to save a life. Do it wholly for the love of God. " Whatever you do, whatever you eat, whatever you give away in charity, do it as an offering unto Me!" the Lord tells Arjuna in the Gita. I do not think there can be a simpler or an easier way of establishing a loving link with Him than this – by offering to Him every act that we do, every word that we utter, and every thought that we think!

6. As you follow the little way, you will gradually reach a stage when it will be perfectly natural for you to turn your back on the world and choose God above all else! God becomes your Father, Mother, friend, Teacher – your constant source of support.

The aspirant who wishes to walk the little way is even like the lotus! Silently it blooms; silently it spreads its beauty and fragrance; silently it grows in beauty, its face ever turned towards the sun! So too, amid the shouts and shows of life, even in the midst of madding crowds, amid constant changes, ups and downs of fortune, the seeker who walks the little way is undisturbed, ever at peace, still as the waters of a lake on a calm and windless day. He grows in blessedness; he flourishes in silence; and whenever he speaks, his words heal and soothe; he has nothing to lose; all he has is his God, and nothing, no one can take God away from him!

The Lord has given us the freedom to choose the path that appeals to us, one which suits our temperament and disposition. Let us choose any path, but let us follow it sincerely. By the grace of God, one day, we shall surely reach the goal and our life will be truly blessed!

Eight Steps On The Path For Beginners

Gurudev Sadhu Vaswani's message for aspirants can be summed up in what I call the blessed eight-fold path. The steps on the path are:

1. Man is a pilgrim, a wayfarer. His pilgrimage is to the eternal, where is his true home. Nothing here belongs to him. Everything is given to him for use. He must use it wisely and well.

2. Man has wandered outside himself. He needs to embark on the interior pilgrimage.

3. He must practise silence everyday and, sinking deeper and deeper within, behold the imprisoned splendour. Sadhu Vaswani's emphasis was more on the unfolding of the heart than on the development of brain power alone. "Awaken thy heart, O man!" he said, again and again.

4. To be able to do so we must annihilate the ego, and walk what Sadhu Vaswani called, "the little way."

5. The non-egoistic man is a picture of forgiveness. He does not remember the hurts that have been inflicted on him.

6. The non-egoistic man has surrendered his will to the Will Divine. He greets every happening with the *mantra*, "I accept!"

7. The heart of such a man is filled with Divine Love. He beholds God face to face.

8. He feels the thrill of the presence of God in all that is around him. And he becomes a servant of those who suffer and are in pain.

Practical Exercise for Beginners

1) Rejoice in whatever God gives you knowing that there is a meaning of mercy in everything that happens. Let this be the rule of your life:

Thou knowest everything, my Beloved,
Let Thy Will always be done!
In joy and sorrow, my Beloved,
Let Thy Will always be done!

2) Preferably at the same time and in the same place, go and sit in silence. Sitting in silence, you can repeat the Name Divine, or engage yourself in an intimate and loving conversation with God, meditate or do your spiritual thinking.

3) Practice the presence of God all the time. He is not from you afar. He is wherever you are. Call Him and He is here beside you.

4) Do not have *dosh drishti* i.e. do not see fault in another. Baha'u'llah said if there is a man who has one virtue and nine vices, do not consider his nine vices but pay attention to his one virtue. If there is a man who has one vice and nine virtues, consider his nine virtues and do not pay attention to his one vice.

5) Each day let us pray: O merciful one, have mercy on me. If you beg for mercy, you must be merciful to all around you. Therefore, be careful about your diet and your dress. You must eschew all food of violence (flesh, fish, fowl) and adopt a vegetarian diet.

6) You must try to see the One Lord in all who cross the pathways of your life. Treat every guest as an *atithi*—a picture of God.

7) If you give anything to the poor, do not feel that you have given anything and done a favour to the poor—it should be the other way round. You should feel grateful to the poor who give you an opportunity to serve them!

Ask Yourself

- What am I sowing in the field of life?

- What will happen to me when I die?

- Do I get puffed up with pride and seek credit for everything I do?

- Am I being swayed by temptations?

- Do I practice silence daily?

- In pursuit of money, am I ignoring my health?

- Do I have any spiritual goals and aspirations in addition to my professional and personal goals?

- What should I do to make my life more meaningful?

Sadhana for the Spiritual Aspirant

We are told a young boy arrived early on a fine morning, to join Guru Nanak Dev's *satsang*, to sing hymns and utter the Name Divine with the older devotees.

Having observed him for days, the Guru called him and enquired affectionately, "A child like you should be fast asleep at this early hour of the dawn. What brings you here to this congregation?"

With folded hands, the young lad said to the Guru, "Holy Master! I gather wood for my mother everyday, so that she may light the household fire. One day I actually saw the fire burning, and I found that the smaller pieces of wood burnt sooner, quicker than the large ones. I thought to myself that I am like those small pieces – and that I may be consumed by the flames, by the fire of death any time. Therefore I have come to you – that I may conquer death before death consumes me."

Guru Nanak was so pleased with the wisdom of the young boy, that he bestowed on him the name – *Bhai Buddha* which means 'Old Brother' or 'Wise Brother'.

Awakening, spiritual aspiration, the impulse to turn away from the allures of the world may come to an individual at any time in his life. When this awakening is accompanied by the determination to tread the seeker's path with full concentration, he becomes a seeker, a spiritual aspirant.

Human life is a bridge we must cross to reach the other side: can anyone be so foolish as to build his house upon a bridge?

We will not linger on the bridge forever – indeed, we must not. He who realises this becomes a true seeker. The true seeker realises that the purpose of this human life is liberation and self-realisation – and therefore, he first seeks to attain the feet of the Guru. He knows this well: that it is only the Guru who can reveal to us our true identity – the *atman* within us.

The seeker, the serious spiritual aspirant starts off as a true disciple!

Who is a true disciple?

Sadhu Vaswani tells us: He who loses himself in his teacher, is the true disciple.

He who follows his own will and his own desires is neither a true seeker nor a true disciple; he who harbours doubts in his heart and is dominated by personal ambition may be intellectually strong; he who argues endlessly and emphasises the rightness of his own point of view may be an able debator – but a seeker he cannot be: for he is a worshipper of himself.

What are the marks of a true disciple, we asked Sadhu Vaswani. The Master outlined the following traits:

1. Humility: When a true disciple was asked whether he was such-and-such-a one's disciple, he answered, "I am *trying* to be his disciple, so help me God."

Humility helps us to avoid several obstacles and evils on the path of discipleship – such as ostentation and pretension.

2. Obedience to the teacher: The disciple must always remember that in obeying his Guru, he obeys God.

The teacher may put the pupil to severe tests. The worst may be this – that he asks the disciple to be far away from him. For a teacher knows that a raw fruit requires both sunshine and shadow, in order to ripen in maturity. So too, the disciple must have the double experience of fellowship and separation: for in separation too, there is union.

Spiritual obedience to the teacher, not physical nearness to him, is the mark of a true disciple.

3. *Seva* or service: the disciple must serve the teacher whole heartedly.

Growing in humility, obedience and service, the disciple will develop intuition and rise to meet his Guru on the *buddhic* plane.

Intuition is the power to see on the inner plane. When this power develops, the disciple does not argue: he easily understands his teacher. The disciple learns to 'feel' intuitively, the wishes of his teacher. The teacher may not utter a single word. So it was that the Master said: "My own hear My voice."

A true disciple becomes less and less argumentative: when his legitimate questions have been answered, his genuine doubts cleared, he becomes more and more intuitive. He loses himself in the Guru.

A man of God was once asked: "What is the way to God?"

He replied, "When thou hast vanished on the way then thou hast come to God!"

So the disciple too, must 'vanish' so that he may become the seeker who is prepared to see the Light!

It is only after the seeker has found a mentor, a man of Light, a Guru, that his spiritual journey begins. Here are a few simple things which we can try to practise in our daily life, when we begin our journey on the path of the seeker, the spiritual aspirant or true disciple:

1) Do not seek pleasure. By this, I do not mean that you should

become an ascetic. You have to live with the members of your family, live with them as one of them. Outwardly, there should appear to be no differences between you and them. It is your *inner* life, inner attitude that should be different.

Do not seek pleasure – do not desire anything. Accept whatever comes to you. If you find that a meal served to you – lunch or dinner – is not to your liking, do not fret and fume, do not complain or criticise. Accept the food as *prasadam* from God.

Sadhu Vaswani taught us, that in moments when we feel we are about to be overpowered by circumstances, it will do us good to whisper to ourselves, "This, too, shall pass away." I have found this to be a very efficacious *mantra* in times of trial.

Is not our life like a river? It flows on and on, and as it flows, it sometimes cuts through green and beautiful landscapes, sometimes through arid, wild, lonely tracts. When it passes through cool, green woods, it does not say, "How beautiful it is here! I shall stop by, and enjoy this scene a little longer!" It flows on. When it has to pass through dreary tracts, it does not say, "I refuse to flow through these parts!" It goes on. Like the river, we too must go on, seeking all the time, the Sea of Life that is God Himself.

2) Do not cling to your possessions. Cultivate what Huxley describes as the spirit of affective poverty – being indifferent to money. This is different from effective poverty – possessing no money.

A man may have no money – and yet within him the craving may be strong for things which money can buy. Another man, like Raja Janak, may have the wealth of the entire Kingdom, and yet be detached from possessions, power or position, which money can bring.

Be detached. If you have an impulse to give something away, give it without hesitation, give it readily and cheerfully. Until we have learnt to give, we cannot grow in spiritual strength.

Jalal-ud-din Rumi speaks of King Ibrahim in whose heart was the longing to see God. But he was still attached to his Kingship. One day, as he was about to fall asleep, he hears footsteps on his roof. Looking out of the window, he calls sharply, "Who goes there?" the answer comes from the rooftop, "I have lost my camels, and I am searching for them."

Half amused and half annoyed, the king cries, "What an idiot you must be, to search for camels on a rooftop."

Back comes the answer: "No worse than you, O king, who, sitting on your throne, tries to seek union with God!"

The king's spiritual journey begins at this point. He renounces his kingdom and sets out to seek the Truth.

Grow in the thought that nothing belongs to you, nothing is really yours. If something you value and cherish is lost or stolen, learn to say to yourself, as the philosopher Epictetus did, in similar circumstances, "I have given it back."

3) Claim nothing for yourself. So learn to give without expecting anything in return.

Give the love of your heart to all who come to you, and if they do not love you in return, let that not put you off.

Ignatius Loyola founded the society of Jesus. He was once asked how he would feel if the Pope were to issue an order for closing down his Society. Loyola, who had by then attained the state of holy indifference to success or failure, said, "A quarter of an hour of prayer, and I should think no more about it."

4) Do not be over anxious about anything, even about your spiritual progress. For remember, He who is our Lord and Master, the *Satguru*, knows what is best for us, and if He wishes us to go slow, He knows best; there must be wisdom in it. Therefore, do not be anxious. To be anxious is to waste a lot of energy which may otherwise be used for a good purpose. Learn to resign yourself in His Will. "Thy Will be Done!" Let this be the one prayer of your

heart. "Not mine, but Thy Will be done, O Lord!"

I have shared with you four simple, spiritual practices that I found useful, when I set out on the path. They are easy to talk about, easy to list – but very difficult to follow, to act and to *be*.

The start of the spiritual life is struggle and striving. We starve – and our hunger cannot be satisfied by the most delicious dishes. We feel thirsty, and our thirst cannot be quenched by the choicest drinks on earth. Our hunger and thirst grow more and more. Then it is, that a yearning heart cries out, "O, for someone who may take me out of this little self into the larger life of the spirit, someone who has drunk the elixir of life and tasted of the Nectar of God's grace."

Such a one, for want of a loftier name, we call Guru. I love to speak of him as the Beloved.

It is your greatest good fortune to come into contact with such a one on the pathways of life. You will look at him, he will look at you, he will look *into* you, he will read your heart as the pages of an open book. Each will recognise the other, and you will hear within your heart, his whisper, "Come, my child! Follow me!" And, without a single question, a single doubt, you will follow him wherever he leads you to the very ends of the earth, even unto hell.

If the search of the worldly man is for the goods of the earth, for pleasure, power and possessions, the quest of the true seeker is for the life of the spirit. It was Jesus, who said: "Seek and ye shall find". By seek, did he not mean, "Seek thy Guru"?

It is only when you have found your Guru that your spiritual journey begins, in earnest. And you do not have to leave your home and wander far and near, in search of such a One. All you need to do is: aspire, aspire!

Aspire that it may be your fortune to draw near to someone, touching whose feet may be to you, a communion with God.

Aspire! Aspire! And aspiration, like the smoke of fire, always rises upward. So let the fires burn within you continually.

Read books, but remember that books will not take you far. Books may, indeed, become a barrier. For there is always a danger of dropping into the pitfall of the vanity of learning. Therefore, read little, and practice more. Let your reading be reflected in your daily life.

And remember – *you* may not find your Guru. But if you seek him, aspire for his grace, *he* will surely find you. And when he does, you will feel, "This is my Guru! He is the one I have been waiting for all these years! My blessed Master, why were you away from me for so long!"

He, in his grace will find you. And it will be his grace, his responsibility to ensure the success of your *sadhana*.

Seven Steps On The Path For The Spiritual Aspirant

1. The secret of the new life is love of God. This love grows more and more with each passing day. Love is a gift of God to man. Therefore, pray as often as you can, "I love you God! I want to love you, more and more! I want to love you more than anything in the world. I want to love you to distraction, to intoxication. Grant me pure love and devotion for Thy Lotus-feet, and so bless me that this world bewitching *maya* may not lead me astray. And make me, Blessed Master, an instrument of Thy help and healing in this world of suffering and pain."

2. There comes a time when we realise that we cannot serve two masters at the same time. A decision has to be taken – either we choose God or the world. We cannot have both. There must be no compromise. The seeker after God stands up for truth – in thought, in speech, and in all his dealings with others. Truth – though she take me to the gallows! Truth though she lead me through the flames!

3. If you have wronged a person, do not waste time in making amends. Have you hurt someone? Have you cheated him? Have you spread scandals against him? Have you exploited him for selfish purposes? Then waste no time in setting right what has gone wrong.

4. Has someone wronged you? Forgive him even before forgiveness is asked. And your mind will be at peace and the world around you will smile back at you.

5. Whatever you do – be it a lowly act such as

sweeping a room or a noble deed such as saving a life – do it wholly for the love of God. "Whatever you eat, whatever austerity you practise, whatever you give in charity, whatever you do, do it, O Arjuna, as an offering unto Me," says the Lord in the Gita. Can there be a simpler way of communing with God than this, that we offer unto Him every little thing we do, every thought we think, every word we utter, every aspiration we breathe?

6. Establish more and more points of contact with God. This will give you soul-rest, and out of you the joy of God will flow to many. Be gentle with all who come to you: they have been sent by God to your door, with a definite purpose.

7. Help as many as you can to lift the load on the rough road of life. Gurudev Sadhu Vaswani once said:—

Did you meet him on the road?

Did you leave him with the load?

On the road of life are many who go about carrying heavy loads. The loads are not merely physical. There are many who carry upon their hearts the loads of worry, anxiety and fear. Lighten their loads. Be their burden-bearer. The day on which we have not helped a brother here or a sister there, a bird here or an animal there – for birds and animals, too, are God's children and man's younger brothers and sisters in the "one family of creation" – the day on which we have not helped someone in need is a lost day, indeed.

Ask Yourself

- Do I choose God or do I choose the world?

- Do I have a hunger and thirst for the life of the spirit?

- Do I seek to please people or do I seek to please my Guru?

- Am I willing to suppress my whims and obey my Guru implicitly?

- Do I serve my Guru whole heartedly?

- How often do I fret and fume, complain and criticise?

- Am I willing to forgive others and let go of the grudges within my heart?

Practical Techniques of *Sadhana*

THE FIRST TECHNIQUE OF *SADHANA:*
SILENCE

Silence is the language of the soul; it is the unspoken, unwritten vocabulary of prayer and devotion; the music of stillness; the mirror of your innermost self. I like to think of silence as our personal, intimate appointment with God. And for those who wish to take up *sadhana* as a way of life, silence is the first and simplest step on the path.

Silence is two-fold; there is outer silence, which is freedom from noise, freedom from the shouts and tumults of daily life; and there is inner silence, which is freedom from the clamour of the senses and desires; it is the cessation of all the mental acrobatics that we are constantly engaged in; it is the quitening of all the conflicting passions and sensations that dominate our mind.

Such a silence, interior silence, in short, gives us the peace that passeth, surpasseth understanding!

Even as particles of dust cling to our clothes, so too, particles of noise, the shouts and clamour of this world, cling to our hearts. We wash our clothes with soap and water to clean them; even so, we must dip our minds and hearts in the cool, clear, purifying waters of silence, to cleanse the interiors. Silence is our own spa-treatment for the spirit. Therefore, it is necessary for all of us to practise silence everyday.

We live in a world where everyone talks far too much. We talk excessively in public and in private. As a wise man put it, "Men seem to feel the need to cloak and excuse their imperfections and wrong deeds in a mass of prattle." We need to devote a few minutes each day to the healing, soothing, purifying influence of silence.

Socrates counselled his disciples to keep their mouths shut – and speak only when absolutely necessary.

"O wise one, how may we know when it is right to speak?" they asked him.

"Open your mouths to speak only after you have asked yourself three questions, and received an affirmative answer to each of the three" replied Socrates.

What are the three questions?

The first question we must ask ourselves before we speak is – is it true? If we are not sure about the veracity of what we are saying, it is better that we do not utter a word. When we utter words carelessly, we ourselves become transmitters of untruth.

The second question to ask is – is it pleasant? Many are the empty remarks and vain statements that people make in idleness to hurt others. It is better that these unpleasant words remain unspoken.

The third question according to Socrates is – is it useful? Is our statement going to benefit the listener? Will our words bring comfort to someone? Are we likely to help someone with what we say? Only in that case should we go ahead and speak.

An Eastern account of Jesus attributes the following statement to him, "A day will come when you will have to render account for every idle word you have spoken."

We will all do well to remember this; we must pay – not merely for an untrue word, not merely for a bitter word, but for every *idle* word we have uttered.

Is it true? Is it pleasant? Is it useful? These are the three questions we must ask ourselves before we speak. Let silence be the law of our life. For silence hurts no one; if you have something to say that is better than silence, then speak those words freely; otherwise, remain silent. If only we could collect all the useless, idle, hurtful words we utter, they would form a veritable mountain of words.

Silence is relaxation for the mind, even as rest is relaxation for the body. It should be our earnest effort, at least once a day, to escape from the stress, strain, tension and turmoil of life, and practise absolute silence. We can easily give up mindless activities like watching TV or gossiping with friends, to devote to the practise of silence.

Silence helps us commune with the inner self. Silence enables us to discipline our petty, calculating intellect. Silence takes us closer to God. In silence, we can feel our prayers reach Him and in perfectly held silence we may even hear His answers to our prayers.

As I said earlier, I call my habitual hours of silence, my "daily appointment with God." It is vital that we cultivate the healing habit of silence in this age of noise and ceaseless activity. In fact, the great need of modern man is silence. To help us to avoid stress and tension, the noted psychologist, Deborah Bright, recommends what she calls PQT – Personal Quiet Time – of twenty minutes, twice a day.

Silence heals; silence soothes; silence comforts, silence purifies, silence revitalises us. In this world of allurements and entanglements, the sharp arrows of desire, craving, animal appetite, passion and pride, ignorance, hatred and greed wound our souls again and again. Our souls bear the scars of many wounds. Silence is the great healer that can heal these wounds.

A doctor I know had to treat a woman patient suffering from a severe throat infection and chest congestion. He wrote out a simple prescription for her: *Complete and utter silence.*

"Did the prescription really work?" I asked him.

"Sure it did," he replied. "The patient was indeed suffering; her symptoms were real but I could not medicate her because I knew her affliction was not physical."

"Did she get better?" I persisted.

"In body, mind and spirit," answered my friend.

Dr. Albert Schweitzer said: "Each patient carries his own doctor inside him. We are at our best when we give that doctor a chance to work on the patient." God has given us all the power of healing ourselves. All we need to do is to allow this power to work – and there is no better way to do this than the practise of silence.

When we shut out the harsh and grating noises of the world – the deafening sound of men, machines, automobiles, strife, arguments and clashes – our hearts and minds are quietened, and we listen to the Divine Harmony within us. It is of this Divine Harmony that Shakespeare writes:

Such harmony is in immortal souls;
But while this muddy vesture of decay doth grossly close it in,
We cannot hear it.

Beautiful and serene is the silence of the spirit. When we enter its realm, we experience peace, harmony and a sense of well-being. Our ego gives way to Divine Love. Our stress and tension melt away. In this condition, we can listen to our inner voice, which can help us solve the most difficult problems of this life.

Have you seen a plant that has not been watered? It's leaves grow pale, its flowers wither, and it droops miserably. The moment you nourish the plant, the leaves will regain their lost freshness and greenness. Gradually, the flowers will recover their beauty and fragrance, and the plant will be restored to life. What you have done is to water the roots, to work this miracle of recovery. Silence waters the very roots of your life. When you open the windows of your heart and soul to receive the silence of the Spirit, you lift your consciousness to bathe in the waters of Divine Healing.

Alas, in the mechanical rush of the modern world, we have lost touch with the cultivation of silence and solitude. Our lives are getting increasingly complicated; the list of things to be done gets longer, while 24 hours seem to get shorter. At the end of the day, we feel drained, exhausted, emotionally and mentally weary. Where can we find retreat from this spiritual exhaustion? The Roman philosopher Marcus Aurelius has the answer: Nowhere can man find a quieter or more untroubled retreat than in his own soul.

It seems to me that many people today are terrified of silence, afraid of being alone. I know several couples who do not like to spend a quiet evening at home, by themselves. They invite friends over, or go over to clubs or to restaurants so that they do not face solitude. I even know a few people in whose homes the TV is always switched on – even when no one is watching it. They tell me it is comforting to hear the sound from the TV.

Why are we afraid of solitude and silence? Possibly because we cannot bear to look deep within ourselves. This is why many people say they don't have time for silence or meditation. But they will realise, when they go deep within themselves, that the Infinite is within – and we have nothing to fear.

When a man sits in silence, he creates a space within himself. In that space he can establish his relationship with God. He can do this by creating beauty in that space – the beauty and glow of love. For most of our waking time, we are pre-occupied with worldly matters; we are isolated from God. We are alienated from our true Home. We exist in a spiritual vacuum.

When we sit in silence, we can connect ourselves with the source of all the universe. If you find this is not happening, you may chant in silence, within your heart, your favourite verses from Holy Scriptures or simply chant silently, the Name Divine.

If you find this also not very congenial, then the easiest thing to do is to sit in silence and write the word *Om*. The point I am making is, that you must withdraw the mind from external worldly temptations and bring it to focus on the inner eye. Then you will find the veil of *maya* is thrust aside, and you glimpse the Truth.

Adi Sankara narrates the following story in his commentary on the *Brahma Sutras*. A guru was approached by a devout disciple who sought to know the nature of the *atman*. Three times, the disciple got the opportunity to have the Master to himself; three times he repeated his question. The Master remained silent for the first and second time; the third time he was asked the same question, he said to the disciple, "I have been teaching you, but you don't seem to follow me. The *atman* is absolute silence. This great truth can be discovered only in the total silence of the mind and heart." Indeed, silence is the language of self-realisation!

As I have said earlier, the first question that the seeker must ask himself is the Socratic query: Who am I? Who are you? Other people have told you many things about yourself — some complimentary, some otherwise. But all that is not really you. You must now try to find who you are. This is the biggest challenge of life. You must discover yourself. It is not easy to do so — but it can be done.

Mullah Nasruddin was out in the street searching for something.

"What are you looking for?" they asked him.

"I have lost my keys," he answered.

"Where did you lose them?" he was asked.

And he said, "I lost them in the house."

Then how is it that you are looking for them here?"

And the Mullah said, "Because in the house it is dark, out here it is so bright!"

We have looked for ourselves out here, but we will not be able to find ourselves until we look within, until we turn inside where it is dark.

Let us practise silence every day, preferably at the same time and the same place — for this is our daily appointment with our own selves, our True Self, the Real Self, the Self Supreme that, for want of a better word, we call God. Begin with fifteen minutes, then gradually increase the period to at least one hour. At first, the practice may appear to be meaningless, a sheer waste of time. But if you persist in it, silence will become alive and the Word of God will speak to you. And you will realise that practising silence is, perhaps, the most worthwhile activity of the day.

God is not from you afar. He is not locked up somewhere in a far-off temple; you do not have to go to a *tapovan* (forest of meditation) or a mountain-peak to find Him. He is *here* – He is *now* – He is in the heart within you. You can speak to Him, commune with Him as with a friend or with a member of your own family. Establish contact with Him in silence – and be prepared to LISTEN – for in the depths of silence will you hear His Divine Voice – not in the clamour and noise of this world.

Silence can give you insight into the self and into your life. It will remind you of the home where you come from, the home to which you must return. It will remind you that you are of the Kingdom of God, that you are bound for the Kingdom of God, and that this Kingdom of God is not from you afar; it is not apart from you; it is an integral part of your being.

Your journey to God is essentially an interior journey. It is a journey in consciousness, a journey of self-awareness. Silence is the process by which you can free yourself, free your consciousness from the lower *chakras*, and raise yourself to the kingdom of God that is within you.

Truth is within! Wisdom is within! The source of all strength is within! Therefore, we must turn within, in silence!

Practical Exercise in Awareness of Silence:

This exercise in silence calms the restless and agitated mind and helps in increasing the power to concentrate on work, studies, and on spiritual development.

Let us relax. Try to relax every muscle, every nerve, every limb of the body – make the body tension-free. Relax the mind as well: let it be free of fear, anxiety, frustration, worry, depression, disappointment. Even as a towel is wrung to drain it of every drop of water, so let the mind, pictured in the form of a towel, be drained of all tension, drop by drop.

We are now ready to embark on a spiritual journey that, with God's grace, will take us into the depths within and give us that which surpasses understanding.

Be relaxed and let the face wear a soft smile.

Let us for a brief while forget the world, forget its worries and vexations, its tensions and tribulations and feel that we are in the presence of God. God is always with us. We are not always with God. We forget Him again and again. Therefore, we must practise the presence of God. Every time we find our thoughts straying away from God, let us bring the mind gently, lovingly back into the Divine Presence. To do this, let us offer a silent prayer: O Lord, may our senses be free from the drag of sense objects. May our minds sit still in the Divine Presence as a bee sucking honey out of a flower.

May our intellect, the *buddhi*, be illumined with the Light of the *Atman*. May our entire being be filled with Light. Light, Light, Light in front, Light behind, Light to the right, Light to the left, Light above, Light below, Light within, Light all around. Light, Light, Light.

Do not interfere with the breathing: merely watch it. Watch the breath as it comes in and flows out at the tip of the nostrils.

This is an exercise in awareness. We do not have to control the breath; we have only to watch it. Be relaxed and let the face wear a soft smile. And be alert.

Remain silent for about five minutes.

The period of silence is over. Rub the palms of your hands together, softly place them on your eyelids, and gently open your eyes. *Om, shanti, shanti, shanti!*

Ask Yourself

- Do I feel the need to relax my mind, just as I relax my body?

- Do I turn on the TV just to avoid the loneliness within me?

- Do I talk more and listen less?

- Do I realise that harsh words can hurt more than sticks and stones?

- Do I feel the need to melt away my stress and tensions?

- Am I afraid of being by myself?

- Am I aware of the price I have to pay for every untrue word that I speak?

THE SECOND TECHNIQUE OF *SADHANA*: FELLOWSHIP WITH SEEKERS – *SATSANG*

The path of *sadhana*, as we saw, is the path of *shreya*: it is not for the idle and the unaspiring souls. We require determination and perseverance to follow this path to its ultimate goal; and the journey is made happy and pleasurable by the fellowship of like minded souls, fellow pilgrims on the path. Even such an invaluable fellowship is offered to us in the guru's *satsang*.

Satsang is a place of hope and serenity; it is a place of positive vibrations, which protect us from the negativity of the world. The temptations of the world are many and the allurements of the world are powerful. Anytime they can drag us into the whirlwind of despair and frustration.

Have you ever wondered what is the noblest thing on earth? Let me answer, in the words of my Gurudev, Sadhu Vaswani, "The noblest work is to cultivate the soul." To cultivate the soul we should sow the seeds of love, selfless service and devotion. We should chant the Name Divine, set apart time for silent communion with God, and offer the service of love to those who are less fortunate than we are. We will then experience Divinity in our everyday life. It is this experience that is offered to us, every day, day after day, in the *satsang*.

I can hear some of my friends exclaim: "Chant the Name Divine? Set apart time for silent communion? Dada, we are not renunciates and ascetics. We are men of the world and we have businesses, careers and families to worry about. What do you want us to do? Take *sanyas* at 35?"

A word of caution to my workaholic friends. It is true that all work is worship of God; and we should put maximum effort into whatever we wish to achieve. But, work should not be killing. It should not drain your spirit or kill you with the slow poison of stress, anxiety and fear. Your work should not cripple you. My dear ones, do not become workaholics; create time for your own self. For, ultimately you have to live for your own self. Allot time for yourself, your spiritual sustenance and growth.

A Saint invited his disciple, who was a busy official, to come and pray with him during his daily *satsang*.

"I wish I could," said the man. "But the trouble is, Master, I am too busy at the moment."

"You remind me of a man walking blindfold in the jungle," said the Master. "And he said, he was too busy to take the blindfold off."

When the official pleaded lack of time, the Master said, "What a sad mistake it is to think that one cannot pray for lack of time."

My friends, you find time for everything else. You attend to your business or profession. You make time for family and friends. You set aside time for parties, picnics and movies. How is it that you cannot set aside 15 minutes out of your busy schedule, to sit quietly and commune with God?

Everyone is busy making money nowadays. They think only of millions, and multi-millions. But you cannot take your millions with you when you leave this world and enter the Great Beyond – as indeed we all must, one day. That day is coming, sure as the sun rises in the east, that day is fast approaching when we will have to leave behind everything – not only all our millions we have made, but also our near and dear ones, family, friends and relatives, our positions, our possessions, our power, all that we have accumulated here. What will we carry with ourselves on that day? What will we take with us when we set out on the inevitable journey?

The *satsang* will give you the answers to all these questions.

Very often when we ask people why they are not attending *satsang* regularly, the reply is, "There is no time" or "I am busy with my work" or "I do not even get time to take a deep breath." and so on. Such excuses cannot fool anyone, not even the people who make these excuses. Some people even say, "Well, when I retire from my active job, I will definitely devote my time to *satsang*, spiritual pursuits and God." But such time rarely comes.

Man's life is so crowded with mundane activities that he rarely has time for self-study and introspection. He seldom finds himself in that expansive, tranquil mood of silence and reflection, where he can listen to God, and chant the Name Divine in the heart within.

The message of every *satsang* is 'go within'. Go within. Explore your interior world and you will find that Divine Light which dispels every darkness.

Who is a true *satsangi*? Not the one who merely attends the *satsang*, but one who absorbs the pure vibrations of the *satsang*, listens to every word carefully, goes home and ponders over the teachings and puts them into practice. At times, hundreds of devotees come to *satsang*, but I cannot help thinking that only a handful among them have true spiritual intentions. But, it does not matter. Some of these devotees will surely reap the benefits of the pure and sacred environment, while the others will make a beginning in the right direction.

Gurudev Sadhu Vaswani often used to tell us that there are three kinds of rains which bring showers of grace upon us in the *satsang*.

The first one is the pure waters of the *satsang*. These Divine Waters flow through *shabad kirtan*, through the sacred words of saints and through the scriptures. They flow from the positive circle of the continuous incantation of prayers and *mantras*. These waters of the *satsang* cleanse your interior, and give you an integration of mind, heart and soul. These waters purify you even as the holy waters of the Ganga cleanse you from within. The waters of the *satsang* are indeed a source of great purification.

The second type of rain is the experience of the interior world, to which *satsang* gives you access. You can contact this source of grace through meditation and silent communion with the Divine, which is offered to you in the *satsang*.

The third type of rain is experienced through selfless service. We all need to have the experience of selfless service. This is like a shower of blessings and joy that invigorates our very spirits. We should spare at least a part of our expenses to be spent in the service of the poor. The waters of selfless service have a magical effect on the body, mind and spirit. It washes away the 'I' of ego. It washes away the cobwebs of the mind and of the lower emotions of the heart. Selfless service washes our inner instrument or *antahkarana*, and leaves us with a lasting feeling of joy that no personal extravagance can ever match.

Selfless service is part of the activities of most spiritual congregations. For beginners, service becomes a happy and easy activity, when undertaken in the company of fellow members of the *satsang*. But we will do well to remember that service should be undertaken with a feeling of devotion. Take it as an opportunity to serve the poor, an opportunity to sublimate yourself, an opportunity to climb one more step towards self growth. Above all do it as an offering to God.

Sadhu Vaswani founded the *Sakhi Satsang* in Hyderabad-Sind in 1929, and later, he formed the Brotherhood Association, with the goal of cultivating the soul. The hundreds of brothers and sisters who flocked to join his spiritual gatherings, gradually became regular *satsangis*. To this day, as many of you know, the *satsang* remains the pivot around which all the Mission activities revolve. Everyday, three *satsang* sessions are held at the Mission Campus, and people make it a point not to miss the daily *satsang*. Some of our Sadhu Vaswani Centres overseas also hold weekly/bi-weekly/daily *satsangs*, which also attract their own share of regular participants.

A friend once expressed his surprise to me, at the fact that people continue to be drawn to the *satsang*, "in this day and age" as he put it. I responded to his remark with the observation that people need the *satsang* today, more than their parents and grandparents did in bygone times.

This is not just my personal opinion. Many *satsangis* tell me, that *satsang* gives them a sense of stability, a positive frame of mind, a certain sense of mental well being and peace of mind. They say that *satsang* links them with a Higher energy and in that positive, joyful atmosphere they feel happy and rejuvenated. Whether they hear discourses or recite prayers or read from the *bani* of great ones or participate in singing the Name Divine, they feel elevated. At such times, their minds are free from worldly cares and anxieties; and there awakens a desire within them, the desire to follow in the footsteps of the truly great ones. They yearn to imbibe the ideals of saints and sages, and make their life more meaningful, more worthwhile.

They say, too, that *satsang* cleanses and purifies their thoughts by its sacred environment and holy vibrations; they are able to discard negative emotions like envy, jealousy, avarice, resentment and anger which trouble all of us at times. In fact, it helps them further by awakening in them the higher impulses that human beings aspire to, such as charity, compassion and philanthropy. And when they yield to these noble impulses, they find that they achieve a sense of harmony and joy that surpasses all worldly satisfaction. In short, they assure me that, *satsang* generates a sense of peace and tranquility, which helps them to evolve into a higher state of living and thinking.

Once, Rishi Narada approached Lord Vishnu and requested him humbly: "My Lord! Do tell me about the value and influence of *satsang*. I am eager to know what it can do for the seeker."

Lord Vishnu smiled at Narada. He said, "I am so busy now, I do not have the time to talk to you about it. But, I would like to help you. Please go to the giant banyan tree in the forest located at the foot of the Meru Hills. There you will find a squirrel. He will enlighten you about *satsang*."

Rishi Narada was puzzled. A squirrel – to enlighten him on *satsang*. But the Lord's word was absolute, and Narada did as he was told. He found the tree in question, and a lively squirrel jumped down before him.

In all respect, Narada said to him, "I pray you, dear squirrel, enlighten me on the value and influence of *satsang*."

The squirrel looked at Narada with its beady, bright eyes for what seemed to be a long drawn out minute. Narada looked into its eyes and held his gaze. At the end of the minute the squirrel curled up, lifeless. It was dead.

Taken aback, Narada found his way back to *Vaikunth*, where he narrated the moving incident to the Lord. "I hope I have not been instrumental in the death of the poor creature," he lamented. "And, dear Lord, my question is still unanswered. Wilt Thou enlighten me?"

"I'm afraid that's not possible Narada," replied the Lord. "Go back to the same tree. You will find a monkey who will give you the knowledge you seek."

Faithfully, Narada did as he was told. Indeed, he found the monkey swinging from one branch to another. When he saw Narada, the monkey jumped down with a thud.

"I pray you, O monkey, to enlighten me on the value of *satsang*," Narada said to the monkey respectfully.

The monkey drew close and looked deep into Narada's eyes. In a minute, he dropped dead at the sage's feet.

This time, Narada was nonplussed. In utter shock, he rushed to Lord Vishnu and said: "Lord, I do not know what is wrong. The monkey you mentioned has also dropped dead before my eyes. What am I doing to these poor creatures? Who will now enlighten me on the *satsang*?"

"Well, Narada," said Lord Vishnu. "Tomorrow a prince will be born in the royal family of the kingdom in which the forest is located. Go and bless the new born child – and he will enlighten you on the matter you seek."

"But... my Lord..." stammered Narada. "When I consider the fate of the squirrel... and the monkey... how can I dare to approach this innocent, newborn baby?"

"Do you or don't you need enlightenment on *satsang*?" asked the Lord with a smile. "Go to the child. Your quest will be fulfilled."

It was with a trembling heart that Narada entered the royal palace the next morning. The King and Queen were deeply honoured to see him. They welcomed him with all ceremony that was due to a *maharishi*. They entreated him to bless their newborn son – the heir to the throne.

Rishi Narada was taken to the room where the baby prince lay asleep in the cradle. His heart beat fast as he laid his hand on the brow of the child to bless him.

No sooner had he touched the child, than the baby opened its eyes and looked deep into the eyes of the Rishi.

"O Prince," said Rishi Narada, a cold sweat breaking out over his forehead. "Lord Vishnu bade me come to you to ask you about the value of the *satsang.*"

To the rishi's utter amazement, the baby began to speak. "Rishi

Narada, you see me here – the manifest proof of the value of *satsang*. In my previous births, I was a squirrel, and then a monkey. As a squirrel, I was only motivated by appetite. I did nothing but gather and hoard. When I met you and looked into your eyes, I was released from that birth. My *karma* caused me to take birth as a monkey. Then again, I had the good fortune to encounter you at close quarters. Released from that incarnation, I have risen in the scale of evolution to take birth as a Prince in the pious family of the King of this country. If one minute in the company of a holy one like you could help me this far, I leave you to judge what the value and influence of sustained *satsang* can be!"

Rishi Narada was overjoyed. The Lord had indeed performed a *leela* to teach his humble devotee the value of *satsang*.

Satsang has a positive effect on man. *Satsang* creates pure and positive vibrations which neutralise the negative emotions of man. When we go to *satsang*, we get to hear discourses of holy men, participate in the recitation of sacred scriptures and singing of soulful *bhajans*. All of this helps to raise the levels of positive vibrations and energises us. For a short time at least, we forget our mundane worries and get immersed in the pure waters of the Spirit. Our emotions rise above the senses, and we cry out, "O Lord! This is bliss. O Lord! You have given me this beautiful gift of life. Till now I have wasted it. But from now onwards, I will strive to achieve the goal of this human birth!"

May I tell you, dear friends, that our life – a little interlude in this world – is part of a Great Design. It is a training ground for self-growth. Very few of us are aware of this purpose. But it is definite that our sojourn on this earth is predestined – perhaps by our own choice – for this life has been given to us for our own spiritual progress and evolution. However, we spend our life in the pursuit of pleasure, thinking that it is the be-all and end-all of our existence. We are so enamoured by the superficial glamour and glitter around us, that we forget the very purpose for which we have come. Daily attendance at the *satsang* will ensure that we do not throw our precious life away in such frivolous pursuits.

It always gives me great pleasure to see young men and women attending the *satsang*. I firmly believe that *satsang* is good for all ages, all stages of man's life. People often make the mistake of assuming that *satsang* is the prerogative of older people, who have more or less withdrawn from active life and wish to have nothing further to do with the world and its affairs. On the other hand, satsang can teach all of us, young and old alike, how to lead our worldly life and conduct our worldly affairs in the right spirit, in the right manner and with the right attitude. We would do well to remember that God's grace is not akin to a pension fund, reserved for senior citizens. It is Grace abounding for us all, now and forever. We do not have to be sixty-five years old to attain God's grace. It came to *Bhakta* Prahlada when he was still a child; it came to Dhruva when he was still a little boy. Age is not a factor that determines our link with God.

People often wonder what exactly goes on in a *satsang*. What are the disciplines prescribed? What is the message of the discourses? What is the message conveyed through them? So let me tell you a little about the Sadhu Vaswani *satsang*. The discourses in our *satsang* are universal in approach. The main teaching given is this: the gift of the human birth so freely bestowed on all of us is invaluable. Saints and sages of all faiths and of all ages have emphasised that human life is God's greatest gift to us. But it is a gift that is meant to fulfill a purpose. It is a rare and valuable gift, and not meant to be wasted on earthly pleasures. It should be used to achieve the ultimate goal – Liberation through service of the Lord, and the suffering children of the Lord.

One of the disciplines we practise in the *satsang* is to sit in silence, meditate and go within the self. For, we believe, that in the practise of silence, we get answers to the most profound questions that vex our minds. In silence we perceive our true selves.

Satsang is nothing but the safest and easiest spiritual routine that we can give ourselves. It cleanses and purifies our hearts. This cleansing of mind and heart is done through the chanting of the Name Divine, associating with men of God, as well as with like-minded aspirants who share our quest for Liberation, through *kirtan, bhajan* and recitations from the sacred scriptures, as well as listening to discourses that enlighten us. Just as we clean our body with soap and water, similarly we can purify our mind and heart by washing them in the waters of the spirit, the *amrit dhara*, that flows perennially in the *satsang.*

Gurudev Sadhu Vaswani gave us an invaluable message, "Your life on this earth is but a journey, a brief sojourn. Your native home lies beyond this earthly plane; and the passage to the native land is through the *satsang.*" The Divine presence of a realised soul, a guru, in itself is a boon, for it brings peace and harmony to your soul, just through the spiritual vibrations that his presence generates. *Satsang* is the flowing water of the spirit. It is the melody of the Name Divine. It cleanses both heart and mind. Therefore, I urge my friends, always join the fellowship of the *satsang* and rejoice in taking dips in the flowing water of the spirit. Do not ever forsake this beautiful, purifying, blissful experience, that is so freely available to all of us. It is as easy as walking in and taking your seat. The power of the *satsang* will take care of the rest.

A sister once came to see me in a very perturbed state of mind. She said that she had been greatly agitated, of late, by a personal crisis that had rocked her life. She needed to talk to me and was anxious for advice. I suggested that as it was nearly time for the evening *satsang,* she should attend the same, and then come to talk to me.

She agreed, and went away to join the *satsang,* which was about to begin. As I remember, it was a Tuesday, which, in our Sadhu Vaswani *satsang,* includes a session of meditation. Every evening when the *satsang* is over, we have a brief session of prayer and silence at Sadhu Vaswani's sacred *Samadhi.* After this refreshing and uplifting session, I sent for this sister myself, for she had indeed appeared very disturbed.

She came running up to me and said, "Yes, Dada?"

I gently reminded her that she had wanted to meet me urgently, over a matter that had been troubling her.

"Oh, yes, I remember," she said, with a smile. "But Dada, I really feel I don't need to trouble you and take away your valuable time now. I have found the answer to my questions, the solution to my problem."

She explained that the moment she walked into the *satsang*, she had felt a sense of peace and calm descending on her. As she heard the *kirtan*, she felt the tears flowing from her eyes, unbidden. The day's *vachan* from the *Nuri Granth*, seemed as if it was just addressed to her. She participated in the *aarti*, which she found to be a healing, purifying experience. In the meditation session which followed, she was actually able to hear her inner voice speak to her, and the terrible weight of anxiety and worry that had been pressing down on her, lowering her morale and her spirit, seemed to lift like a cloud. At the end of the session, she literally felt that she was a new person, ready to take on the blows and buffetts of life. She had not only received inner guidance to approach her own problem, but was also filled with a sense of well-being, courage and confidence. In fact, till I sent for her, she had almost forgotten that she had come to me earlier that evening, in a distraught condition, seeking answers to questions that overwhelmed her. Such was the effect of *satsang* on her!

Indeed, I can vouch for the fact that *Satsang* is an abundance of positive energy. We must all avail of it.

In the *satsang*, we get associated with a man of God and he blesses us with spiritual treasures. Truly speaking, triple is the treasure that one receives from a man of God. However, we should go to a *satsang* with an emotional yearning and a thirst for spiritual knowledge. The yearning should be deep, as deep as when floundering in the darkness, one yearns for a ray of light. Go to *satsang* with devotion, with love, with yearning and you will receive the triple treasure of spirituality.

What are these three treasures that we receive from *satsang*?

The first treasure is that we learn meditation. Sitting at the lotus feet of a holy one, we learn to meditate. Meditation stills our restless mind. The treasure of meditation / concentration is found only by those *satsangis* who go there with true devotion. It is said, "Through concentration, you will experience bliss." First we learn concentration. And then we move to meditation, which takes us to the higher regions of Awareness and Bliss.

The second treasure which we receive is *Naam Kirtan*. By chanting the Name Divine, by immersing ourselves into the holy waters of the spirit, we are relieved of many tensions. By chanting the Name Divine, our *antah karan* – inner instrument gets purified; it draws our senses to a focus, and we feel refreshed.

The third treasure which we receive from *satsang* is prayer. What is prayer? Prayer is contact with the Unseen. It is the link to the Universal Self. Prayer helps us to build a relationship with the Invisible. Prayer is a rare treasure and he who knows to pray is truly blessed.

How can we gather to ourselves the true treasure of *satsang*? So let me give you a few practical suggestions:

1. Seek the company of people who go to the *satsang*. Association with them will give you the impulse to enter the world of the *satsang*, a world of spiritual quietude and prayer.

2. Take care of your leisure activities like reading and TV. Very often, the forms of 'entertainment' you choose can be detrimental to your personal growth. Those who read the biographies and the teachings of the great ones are more drawn to the *satsang*.

3. Set apart some time everyday to refrain from worldly activities and focus on the inner world within you. Enter into nurturing activities like meditation, recitation from the scriptures, etc.

4. Keep yourself away from all unproductive talk, gossip and controversies. Do not criticise others, nor entertain gossip about them.

5. Do not miss your daily appointment with God. Fix a time for your silence. Resolve that you will sit in silence for 15 minutes or half an hour or an hour. During this period you can chant the Name Divine, you can commune with God, meditate on some inspirational teachings, or pick up a sentence from a spiritual literature on compassion, oneness, etc. and reflect on it.

Ask Yourself

- Am I a workaholic?

- Will I be able to carry my wealth and possessions to the great beyond?

- Am I blowing away my precious life in frivolous pursuits?

- Do I want to experience the joy and peace that can uplift me to higher planes?

- Is my life so crowded with mundane activities that I rarely have time for myself?

- Do I want to wean away from the negative and invigorate myself in a positive environment?

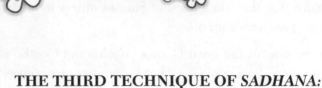

THE THIRD TECHNIQUE OF *SADHANA:* REVERENCE

Reverence is one of the vital attributes that the seeker on the path needs to cultivate. Reverence is the secret of true *sadhana*.

The Law of Reverence is fundamental to the Hindu way of life. It is the law of *shraddha*. The essence of the Vedas – what we call Vedanta – teaches us that there is but One Life in all! The One Life permeates the entire Universe and all of creation. The One Life sleeps in the mineral and in the stone, stirs in the vegetable and in the plant, dreams in birds and in animals and wakes up in man. Therefore, it is incumbent upon every Hindu to respect, revere life in all its myriad forms.

Reverence for life, let me add, is also the fundamental concept of ethics. Its one essential rule, its one *sadhana*, is that *I give myself for other lives*. For all life is sacred, even the life of savages, of primitive people, of uncivilised ones, of wild jungle men, of the criminal, the robber, of the bird and the beast. All life is sacred. All life has its claims on every one of us. True ethics, therefore, rests on recognition of this thought – the reverence for life.

Reverence for life includes (1) sympathy or fellow-feeling and, (2) something more, i.e. love. Reverence for life is love for all living beings – the whole universe. This reverence makes it imperative on us not to cause pain to anybody – pain by thought, pain by word, pain by deed. When I guard my words, deeds and thoughts, to ensure that they do not cause pain to others in any way, I am practising reverence for others.

Reverence, as the great German world-poet Goethe said, is of three aspects: Reverence for what is above us, reverence for what is around us and reverence for what is below us. Reverence for the vast universe that God created; reverence for the great ones of humanity; reverence for the poor and needy; reverence for the speechless world of birds and animals – this is what will enable us to be liberated from the vain and empty cult of the ego – and this, we must aim to achieve. For true liberation is emancipation from the ego; and I repeat these beautiful words from our scriptures: *Ya vidya sa vimuktyate – that* is true knowledge, which liberates us!

It was the poet Tennyson who penned those memorable lines, which I love to quote again and again:

Let knowledge grow from more to more,
But more of reverence in us dwell!

If there is one quality which is sadly lacking in our lives today, it is the beautiful virtue of reverence: reverence for what is above us, reverence for what is around us, and reverence for what is below us.

It is with good reason that the spiritual path is described as a tough and demanding one, while the worldly path of the unthinking, unawakened human being is referred to as "the primrose path of dalliance." It is far easier to live a life of mindless pleasure, than to cultivate the spirit in quest of liberation. Let me repeat, the spiritual path is difficult. There are many obstacles on the way. Even when you have scaled the heights, there is ever present, a danger of falling off the peak. To remain safe and secure in spiritual attainment, one needs the protection of the Guru or the grace of God. To rid yourself of delusions of grandeur, to realise your own limitations, and to seek the constant guidance of a preceptor or Guru, and live in obedience to his teachings, in utter dependence and humility, is to walk what Sadhu Vaswani called the 'little way'. There is no heroism involved here; only reverence for the guru, utter humility and complete self-surrender.

I have always asserted that Hinduism is not a religion, but a way of life. And the Hindu way of life embraces the whole of God's creation in its entirety. "All that is, is a vesture of the Lord," proclaims the *Isa Upanishad*. The concept of the Brahman, or Universal Soul, encompasses the entirety of existence. Since all aspects of existence are part of this Universal Soul, Hindus believe that the Divine is manifested in every living being. This leads to the ideal of reverence for all life, and its corollary, *daya* or compassion, and *ahimsa* or non-violence.

My vision of fellowship and brotherhood shows me a world in which the right to life is accorded to every creature that breathes the breath of life. How can wars cease until we stop *all* killing? How can we claim to seek world peace when we continue to slaughter sentient creatures? For if a man kills an animal for food, he will not hesitate in killing a fellow man whom he regards as an enemy! Therefore, I urge on my friends, the practise of vegetarianism.

Reverence for nature is essential. Reverence for nature will help us to survive upon this planet. Reverence for nature will help us to preserve and protect this blessed earth for our children—and our children's children.

Reverence is essential—reverence for our rivers and forests; reverence for our lakes and waterfalls; reverence for trees and plants and the grass that grows beneath our feet; reverence for birds and beasts, whom I love to call our younger brothers and sisters.

Sadhu Vaswani spoke to us of the *Prakriti Sangha*—fellowship with nature—which he believed was essential to human happiness. There is a spiritual element in the beauty of nature, for nature is God's own expression in all its joy. It is the song, the dance of the

Lord. Nature is truly the environment of the *atman*—the eternal soul within each human being.

I remember, I was out on a walk with Sadhu Vaswani one day – may I say, in the days of my youth, "when I was green in judgement." On the way, a midsize stone lay on the pavement, across our path. Anxious that it should not obstruct the Master's steps, I hastily kicked the stone aside.

Sadhu Vaswani was deeply pained—and I was puzzled. Why should he be hurt that I had put aside a stone? After all, it was only a stone.

I got my answer, in words that I will never, ever forget: "If God is in the scripture, is He not in the stone?" the Master said.

God dwells in all nature—therefore, let us cultivate reverence for nature.

Reverence for those around us involves treating everyone we come across with equal respect and avoiding all forms of exploitation. Several forms, several modes, several degrees of exploitation exist in our world today. Exploitation is the utilisation of something or someone's services in an unjust, cruel or selfish manner for one's own advantages. If a transaction is mutually advantageous, it ceases to be exploitative.

In social and economic terms, exploitation involves a transaction in which a group of people are persistently and unfairly mistreated for the benefit of others. Thus, slavery was one of the worst forms of human exploitation.

In ethical terms, exploitation involves the treatment of human beings as mere 'objects' or as merely a means to serve others' ends. People are regarded as *resources* for utilisation without any consideration for their welfare or well-being.

Child labour is one of the worst forms of exploitation. It refers to the employment of underage children as part of a regular work force. This happens in factories, quarries, agriculture, hotels, small businesses and restaurants. We are now beginning to hear also of children being forced to join military outfits. This is something all of us should be ashamed of!

I am of the firm opinion that all our transactions, all our relationships, should be based strictly on the principle of justice. For exploitation, in the long run, leads only to hatred and conflict.

Animal abuse is yet another form of exploitation. This involves cruelty to animals, and causing them unnecessary harm and suffering. Personally, I feel that factory farming and even animal testing are barbaric practices, unworthy of any evolved civilisation. For me, cruelty to animals is a *moral* issue.

There are people who speak up against all other forms of exploitation, and you will forgive me if I voice my support for the dumb and defenseless creatures. They have no press, no TV, no media, no spokesperson to voice their grievances. They need friends, they need spokespersons.

In my humble opinion, the true seeker who wishes to tread the path of *sadhana*, should avoid all forms of cruelty, all forms of exploitation in his daily activities. The Buddhist thinker Thich Na Hanh warns us: "Do not live with a vocation that is harmful to humans and nature. Do not invest in companies that deprive others of their chance to live. Select a vocation that helps you realise the ideal of compassion."

Truer words were never spoken. Unless we are alert and vigilant, we will find ourselves offending the cardinal Rule of Right Livelihood. When we practise a profession that harms either human beings or nature, we are inflicting physical and moral harm on them and ourselves.

You may argue that we live in a world where jobs are difficult to find. If I refuse to work with harmful chemicals, pesticides, or in the manufacture of arms and ammunition, I may have to remain unemployed. Alas! Many of us do not see this clearly enough.

Many of us are too cowardly to speak out. Such issues should be discussed at a global level and new jobs should be created that are humane and responsible for the welfare of society. For example, consider the irony of Western nations manufacturing weapons to sell to poor Third World countries, while people in these countries are starving for lack of food.

Every year in Pune, we organise a Peace March in connection with my Beloved Master's Birthday (Nov. 25), which is celebrated as International Meatless Day and Animal Rights Day. Every year, people ask me the same question: What has meat-eating to do with world peace?

My answer is always the same: "All killing is a denial of love. For to kill or to eat what another has killed, is to rejoice in cruelty. And cruelty hardens our heart and blinds our vision, and we see not, that they whom we kill are our brothers and sisters in the one brotherhood of life!"

Observing even one day in the year as Meatless Day helps many people to become vigilant and aware of the cruelties that are perpetrated on animals day after day. Indeed, I am happy to tell you that quite a few people who pledged to go meatless for one day, have subsequently abstained from all food of violence for a lifetime.

"As a man thinketh, so he becomes," is the immutable law of human nature. Fill your mind with thoughts of joy, love, peace and harmony – these aspects will be reflected in your external life. Love and peace and joy will then flow out from you to others in an endless stream.

Here are the ten methods recommended by Zen Master Liao-Fan Yuan to cultivate the spirit of reverence and goodwill to all:

- Benefit others in all that you do. Think about the welfare of all

- Treat people with respect and love, no matter who they are and what they do

- Help others, provide them with opportunity to do good
- Encourage others, inspire others by your example, to do good
- Help people in misfortune
- Support public works that are meant for public good
- Give of your material wealth generously
- Protect and support all spiritual teaching
- Respect your elders
- Protect all forms of life

Ask Yourself

- By inflicting pain on others am I inviting pain for myself?

- Do I like to be treated with love and respect? Should I not treat others similarly?

- What if I was the animal being slaughtered, cut into pieces and cooked for someone's meal?

- Do I exploit others or take undue advantage of them?

- Can I give life to a dead creature? Then how can I take away the life of one?

- Do I invest or work in companies that deprive others of their chance to live?

THE FOURTH TECHNIQUE OF *SADHANA:*
CONCENTRATION

Concentration is the ability to focus vision, thought and mind in a unified function. It is an essential attribute to the seeker who wishes to undertake serious *sadhana*.

Have you heard of this beautiful incident in the *Mahabharata*, where Guru Dronacharya is teaching his royal pupils to concentrate their attention on the chosen target? He points to a parrot, perched on the green and leafy branch of a tree, completely camouflaged by the greenery all around. One by one, the Kaurava and Pandava princes are asked to come under the tree and take aim at the parrot: only to take aim, *not* to shoot their arrows.

Each prince comes as the Guru calls out his name. Each strings his bow, fixes his arrow, and takes aim.

"What do you see?" asks the Guru of each one, as he stands beneath the tree and looks up at the bird.

"I can see the green leaves fluttering in the wind," one replies.

"The glare of the sunlight through the leaves almost blinds me," says another.

And so they come and go; one can hardly see the parrot for the leaves; another sees glimpses of the blue sky *above*; one complains that the bird is barely visible.

"I can see its sharp, brown claws and its pointed, red beak clearly!" exclaims Duryodhana. "I see the bird clearly!"

The last to take aim is Arjuna, the Guru's favourite disciple. He too comes and takes aim, looking up steadily, directly.

"What do you see?" the Guru asks again.

"I see only the eye of the parrot," Arjuna replies.

"What else do you see?" the Guru asks. "Can you see the leaves, the sunlight trickling through the leaves, from the blue sky beyond?"

"I can see none of these," replies Arjuna. "I can only see the eye of the parrot."

This is concentration – The ability to focus vision, thought and mind in a unified function.

The Chinese sage Chuang–Tzu relates an interesting story. There was a man who used to forge swords for the Minister of War. He was eighty years old – and yet his work was perfect. He never once slipped.

The Minister of War once asked him, "Is it just your inborn ability, the skill you have acquired or is it the method you follow?"

"It is none of these," the old man replied. "It is just concentration. I started forging swords when I was twenty years old. I cared for nothing else. If a thing were not a sword, I simply did not notice it. I just gave all my energy and effort and attention to making swords."

Concentration has been defined by a wise teacher as wholeness, unity and equilibrium – a unification of the senses and the faculties. They must work in unified harmony.

Meditation is not possible without concentration. And I don't just mean lower levels of concentration such as we use at work or in the laboratory. I mean the kind of higher concentration in which the mind gathers its full strength through singleness, becoming steadfast and focused, attaining union with the One. This is what Socrates refers to when he says, "Thought is best when the mind is gathered into herself and is aspiring after true being."

The practise of unified, single-minded focus on one subject, is concentration. When it is turned inward, it becomes meditation. As Sri Krishna tells us in the Bhagavad Gita: "As a lamp placed in a windless spot does not flicker, nor does a *yogi* of subdued mind practising union with the self."

When the mind becomes truly focused, we enter into a new dimension of consciousness. "Seeing Self by the self, we are satisfied in the Self alone." When our mind touches the Supreme, it kindles the inner flame and we become illumined souls. For, as the philosopher Plotinus says:

"… it is not possible to see Him or be in harmony with Him while one is occupied with anything else. The soul must remove from itself everything, that it may receive the One alone, as the One is alone."

This oneness with the One, is what we hope to achieve through concentration and meditation.

A Simple Exercise In Concentration:

Our lives need to be renewed, if possible, daily – through contact with God. The rain of God's mercy pours everyday; and those of us who receive it are washed clean, renewed and re-strengthened for the struggles of life. May I suggest to you a simple exercise? Every morning, as you sit in silence, close your eyes and imagine the Life of God coursing through every part of your body, filling it through and through. The Life of God is in us already: we have to be conscious of it. Say to yourself: *Every moment the Life of God* – call Him by what Name you will, Krishna, Buddha, Christ, Guru Nanak: they are all so many names of Him who is Nameless – *is filling every nerve and cell and fibre of my being.*

Then begin with the head. Feel the Life of God coursing through your head, and say, "The Life of God is renewing, revitalising my entire brain, every nerve and nerve centre, and the entire cerebro-spinal-system. And my brain thinks the thoughts of God. It thinks in obedience to the Moral Law.

"The Life of God is renewing the entire sensory system. It is revitalising the eyes; and now my eyes see more clearly, more purely. God's Light shines in and through them: and God's light is the light of purity.

"God's Life is revitalising my ears. They hear more clearly and they hear words that are good and noble; and they hear the music of God that thrills the universe from end to end...

"God's Life is revitalising my nose…. God's Life is revitalising my throat. How sweetly it sings the Name of God and the songs of the saints of God. And it utters words that are sweet and true and helpful to humanity."

Now pause for a moment. Then take in a deep breath and turn your attention to the lungs and the heart. Imagine the Life of God renewing, revitalising, the chest and the heart. "The heart is the seat of emotions, and because God's Life is in it, I shall be emotionally balanced, calm and serene in every situation and circumstance of life."

Turn your attention to your arms and hands. They are the hands of God. They are instruments of God's help and healing in this world of suffering and pain. Think of the stomach and other organs. Then come to your legs, knees, and feet. The feet are now firmly set on the path of righteousness and self-realisation.

After covering your entire body, concentrate once again on the heart. The heart is the Sanctuary of the Temple, the Abode of the Lord. And now imagine the Lord seated in the heart for that is where He is already – His Love, His Wisdom, His Strength, His Intelligence, His Joy, His Peace, all centred there and reaching out to every part of your body and outside to your near and dear ones, and to your friends and "foes" alike.

It will take you longer to read this than to put this simple exercise into practice. Repeat this exercise, as often as you can, during the day. But do it at least twice every day – in the morning and at night. And you will soon, very soon, see the effects of it. Your health will improve. Your mind will be more relaxed and alert. Your heart will be more responsive to the pain of others. And you will grow in fuller, richer, deeper consciousness of the presence of God. He will be more real to you than the things of this earth. New love and longing for Him will wake up within your heart. And you will aspire to dedicate all you are, and all you have, at His Lotus Feet for the service of suffering creation. You will live and move and have your being in the Joy and Peace of God. You will be blessed among the children of men.

Ask Yourself

- Does my mind jump restlessly from one thought to another?

- Am I capable of focusing on any topic seriously and continuously?

- Do I want to experience true peace and tranquility?

- Are my energies dissipated on irrelevant activities or thoughts?

- Do I want to be a slave to my mind and its whims, or to be its master?

- Can I focus my mind to accomplish my goals?

- Do I aspire to be an illumined soul?

- Do I seek to be revitalised and energised with God's power?

THE FIFTH TECHNIQUE OF *SADHANA*: MEDITATION

The word "meditation" is derived from the Latin root which means "to heal". The healing, calming, de-stressing technique of meditation is essential to the seeker on the path of *sadhana*.

Some scholars say that the root of the word 'meditation' is similar to the root of medicine and medicate – which means "paying attention to" something. When we meditate, we pay attention to those depths in our being which are not known to the people outside – which are, perhaps not familiar even to ourselves! Thus, meditation has been described as a process of inner attention.

Psychiatrists as well as spiritual teachers now agree that there are three states of consciousness in all of us: the conscious mind with which all of us are familiar; the subconscious, which is the hidden but powerful part of our psyche, with which we connect only during sleep; the super-conscious which represents the highest degree of awareness that we are capable of. It is the source of the brightest light, the highest power of which we are capable. Meditation is the process in which we establish contact with our super-consciousness.

While many regard meditation as a difficult art, it is actually quite simple. Meditation is directing our attention to the Eternal and keeping it there for a while. Within every one of us is a realm of peace, power, perfection. Through practice, we can, at will, enter this realm and contact God. When we do so, we become conscious of infinite power, a wondrous peace, and realise that everything is perfect and in its own place.

To know what meditation is, we need to go within ourselves and, in the words of Sadhu Vaswani, "sink deeper and deeper". No one else can do that for us; we need to do it ourselves. We need to strip ourselves of all pride and passion, selfishness, sensuality, and sluggishness of soul. We need to remove veil after veil until we reach the inner most depths and touch the Pure White Flame.

There are several reasons why meditation is essential to the seeker in the modern context:

- The unbearable stress and strain of contemporary life needs to be countered with conscious stress-reduction techniques. Meditation is the most effective among them.

- The mind needs to be cleansed of the clutter of accumulated negative thoughts and pressures. Meditation empties the mind and energises the nervous system.

- Meditation strengthens our creativity and inner sense of harmony.

- It increases what the Zen Masters call "mindfulness" – awareness of the *here-and-the now* – so that we get the best out of ourselves and our life, every moment.

- Meditation enhances our powers of love and forgiveness and understanding.

- It makes peace and calmness, the natural condition of our minds.

- It teaches us to stop looking *outward* for our wants, needs and desires; it focuses our attention *inwards*, where lasting peace and joy are to be found.

- It is the best known cure for restlessness and fragmented thinking.

- It brings steadiness to our mind, improving our powers of concentration and memory.

- It helps us avoid the two extreme states of single-minded obsession (monomania) and multi-minded distraction, both of which disturb the mind, thus closing many avenues of insight and wisdom that will be available to us.

- It stabilises the senses and teaches the value of introversion.

- It educates us to become tolerant, patient, understanding and sympathetic individuals.

- As we evolve on the path of *sadhana*, meditation opens possibilities of vital spiritual experiences. These are not just confined to out-of-body, or floating experiences, but deeply intuitive experiences that make us aware of the higher dimensions of life, leading us on to the highest reality.

Like all spiritual experiences, meditation is something that cannot come to us from without. It is true, in the early stages of our spiritual unfolding, the "exterior" life, in a large measure, does shape the "interior" life. What we think and feel, what we read and hear, what we do and speak during the day, is echoed within us in the hours of silence. So it is that we must take the greatest care of our outer life. We must keep watch over our thoughts and feelings, our aspirations and desires, and our words and deeds.

Meditation is gazing inward by opening another aperture of the mind. It is turning away from all outer objects to seek Him whom the Rishis call *Ekamevadvityam* — the One without a second, the One and Only Reality. Meditation is entering upon the interior pilgrimage in which layer after layer of unreality is to be torn. The pilgrim, therefore, proceeds by negation: *neti, neti,* not this, not this! These are not God: I seek Him alone!

The pilgrim enters, more and more, into silence. In silence, he understands the secrets of true freedom. In silence, he makes the discovery that he is not a creature bounded by space and time. He is a child of Eternity: and Eternity is here and now. He is not the isolated creature he thought himself to be. He is a "wave of the unbounded deep." He is one with all life, all creation. He is in all: all are in Him.

As we sit in silence, let us think of a world that is very much like this world but that is free of all disorder and chaos – a world in which everything is done for love's sake, where everyone else, where everything comes to pass in the right way, at the right time, in a perfectly harmonious manner. As we do this, we will find the perfection and peace of God flowing into our lives like a perennial river.

Meditation is not an achievement or distinction that we seek to add to our credit rating. The only reason we choose to meditate is to fulfill a deep thirst, a powerful aspiration in us. The wealth and values of this world do not give us the peace we crave. Worldly achievements and success do not give us a true sense of fulfillment. Like Goethe, we call out, "Light! more light!" Meditation leads us to the Light of all lights.

Let me also warn you, meditation is not mere escapism. If we wish to run away from our responsibilities, duties, commitments and obligations, as well as our problems and sufferings, meditation is not the answer. Our frustrations and failures and disappointments will not equip us to take on the spiritual discipline that meditation requires.

Meditation is a process of self awakening through which we connect ourselves to God. *Dhyana Yoga*, as it is called is nothing but establishing our rightful union with God, as God's children. It enables us to be receptive to God's Voice, which can only be heard in inner stillness. In His voice is true wisdom; in His message to us is true Peace. Meditation leads us on to this Divine Peace.

Meditation is not the same as reflection, contemplation or

introspection – though all of these may be useful aids in preparing for meditation. Some people even spend hours with closed eyes, fantasising; or staring vacantly with open eyes, daydreaming. These are certainly not to be confused with meditation.

Some people describe meditation as an art; others call it a science. It would be truer to say that it is a process or technique by which we link ourselves with the highest state of "awareness" or "consciousness" that we can reach.

Meditation is the best way to attain self-knowledge which is perhaps the highest 'knowledge' that man can aspire to. By self-knowledge I do not mean a SWOT Analysis of your personality – but an introduction to your true self. When you know yourself, you realise your potential and widen your possibilities. Therefore, meditation can also be an effective instrument to help you transform your life by enriching your creativity, and adding to your sense of harmony and happiness.

Meditation is not strenuous or difficult or complicated; when it is practised under proper guidance, it is a peaceful, relaxing process which helps ease stress of body and mind. Therefore, meditation is therapeutic even during its earliest stages. It is the best antidote to stress and tension.

Meditation is not an 'interior monologue' or an inner conversation with yourself. It is not even a system of thought – clarification or seeking solution to a problem. Rather, it is an effort to achieve single-minded, one-pointed focus of awareness – what the Gita describes as *ekagrita*.

Meditation is not emptying the mind of all thoughts – for that is impossible for us to achieve. Rather, through meditation, we try to focus our mind on a single point or object which will enable us to reach deeper into our super-consciousness. In this process of unitary focus, relief is automatically brought to the mind from its habitual stresses, strains and tensions.

Meditation disciplines the mind, sharpens concentration and improves memory. It also energises body and mind. Thus, modern medical practioners have begun to use it as an effective aid in healing and therapy.

Meditation also helps the mind to relate to our inner instinct – intuition, as it is called. This connection aids our creativity and innovative thinking. Thus, meditation is a systematic method of tapping human brilliance.

To grow in the inner life, the life of the Spirit, we need to withdraw from the outer world of noise and excitement. Therefore, we stress the practice of silence everyday. Each day, we must spend some time—at least an hour—in silence. At the very start, perhaps, it will be difficult to sit in silence for an hour at a stretch. Then it would be well if we practise silence for about a quarter of an hour, four times a day.

In due course, the mind will become calm and clear as the surface of a lake on a windless day. Such a mind will become a source of indescribable joy and peace. Significant are the words of the Upanishad: "The mind alone is the cause of man's bondage: the mind is also an instrument of man's liberation."

Simple Exercises in Meditation:

1. This simple exercise will be very helpful to beginners. Let us imagine the mind in the form of a room. In this room let us select a corner and sweep it clean. Then let us sit in the corner and quietly watch the antics and acrobatics of the mind. If only we can dissociate ourselves from them, we shall have thrown off the yoke of the mind. We shall have broken the tyranny of the "ego", which is the only hurdle between us and our God: We shall have grown into that true awareness that, in the midst of our daily duties, my heart is kept fixed on the One Divine Reality.

2. Yet another exercise can be found very helpful. As I sit in

silence, let me offer my mind at the Lotus Feet of the Lord. Every time I find the mind flying off on a tangent, let me quickly and gently bring it back to the Lotus Feet. If, for a whole hour, I have done no more than bring the mind back to the Lotus Feet every time it has moved afar, I have not spent the hour in vain. Gradually, the mind will be tranquilised and I shall taste and know how sweet it is to sit in silence.

3. Sitting in silence, let me repeat the Divine Name or meditate on some aspect of the Divine Reality or on an incident in the life of a man of God. God, it is true, is Nameless: but the sages have called Him by many Names. Choose any Name that appeals to you: repeat It again and again. Repeat the Name—yes, but not merely with the tongue. Repeat It with tears in the eyes. Repeat It until you can repeat It no longer, until you disappear from yourself, your "ego" is dissolved, and you sit in the presence of the Eternal Beloved.

4. We may, also, meditate on some form of God—on Krishna or Christ, on Buddha or Nanak, on a Saint or a Holy One. God is the Formless One: but for the sake of His devotees, He has put on many Forms and visited the earth. Choose any Form that draws you: meditate on It. There should, however, be no attachment to the Form: all Forms, ultimately, have to be left behind. Significant are the words of Meister Eckhart: "He who seeks God under a settled Form lays hold of the Form, while missing the God concealed in it." Meditate on the Form to which you feel drawn, and then go beyond it. Enter into the Form to meet the Formless One!"

The Buddha speaks of five types of meditation. The first is the meditation of love in which we so adjust our heart that we wish for the happiness of all living things, including the happiness of our enemies.

The second is the meditation of compassion, in which we think of all beings in distress, vividly representing in our imagination their sorrows and anxieties so as to arouse a deep compassion for them within us.

The third is the meditation of joy, in which we think of the prosperity of others and rejoice with their rejoicings.

The fourth is the meditation on impurity, in which we think of the evil consequences of immortality, corruption. In this meditation, we realise how trivial is the pleasure of the moment and how fatal are its consequences.

The fifth is the meditation on serenity, in which we rise above love and hate, tyranny and oppression, wealth and want, and regard our own fate with impartial calm and perfect tranquility.

Practical Suggestions

➢ Some people find it easier to meditate after a shower or a bath. Pious *brahmins* perform the *sandhya vandana* regularly after their bath – and this includes the practise of *pranayama* and the recital of the *Gayatri Mantra*. This is obviously because cleanliness of the body is associated with purification of the inner instrument.

If you are unable to have a shower or bath, you can wash your face, hands and feet before you sit down to meditate.

➢ You should wear clean, light, comfortable clothes that are not too tight or restrictive.

➢ It is not recommended to start your meditation after a large meal.

When you have just eaten a main meal, the body systems are focused on the process of the digestion. The subtle nerves of the body become heavy, and your consciousness will not be alert and awake – not at its best.

Many experts suggest meditating on an empty stomach. But

then again, hunger will hinder your concentration. The ideal time would be *atleast two hours* after a meal. Obviously, an early morning meditation will nullify these problems.

➤ If a disturbing, noisy environment prevails, it is best to postpone your meditation. Instead, you can read a holy book, recite a prayer or do *naam-japa*.

➤ Some aspirants find it refreshing and vitalising to meditate occasionally, in the midst of nature. But this cannot be done on a regular basis. For 'meditation' is really a process of 'interiorisation'. Swami Paramahansa Yoganand called this "shutting off the sense telephones". Our ancient sages called this stage *pratyahara* – gathering the scattered forces of the mind.

Beginner's Meditation in Six Simple Steps

This meditation lasts 15 to 20 minutes. It is a meditation of 6 steps. Each step will take roughly 2 and a half minutes to about 3 minutes.

Sit in a relaxed posture. As far as possible, the back, the neck and the head should be in a straight line. In the beginning you may find it difficult to bring them all in a straight line, but do it as far as possible. Above all, be relaxed. Relax your body, relax your muscles, relax your limbs. And now, let us embark on this interior journey – a journey that takes us within – a journey that, in due course, may change our life and fill us with tranquillity, with peace and bliss and make us instruments of God's help and healing in this world of suffering and pain.

1. The first step is the step of rhythmic breathing – therefore breathe in slowly, easily, evenly, deeply, as deeply as possible. And to make your breathing deep, one thing that will help you is, when you exhale, try to breathe out as much as possible. Now take the first step. Empty the lungs as far as possible. Now inhale – take in the breath and utter the sacred syllable, *Om* silently. Then exhale – take out the breath and as you do so, utter the sacred syllable *Om* orally – with sound. Begin. Inhale. Exhale O...M. O...M. O...M. O...M. O...M. O...M. O... M. O...M. O...M.

Some of you feel so relaxed and at peace that you would love to be in this state for a longer period. When you do your individual meditation, you can increase this period.

2. Now we come to the second step. It is the step of detached observation. Detach yourself from the mind. Watch the movements of the mind. Don't get involved with the mind. You are not the mind, you are only a silent observer. Watch the mind without any judgement. Do not judge. This is very, very important. Only observe the mind. Watch the movements of the mind, watch them, don't get involved with the mind. You are not the mind, you are only a silent observer. Watch the movements of the mind even

as you would watch the movements of a little child who is being naughty. Don't pay attention to your breathing. Only watch the movements of the mind. Just watch the mind sitting easily in a relaxed posture, watch what the mind is doing.

Silence

Don't pay attention to the breathing. Only watch the movements of the mind. Watch as a silent observer. Watch without judgement.

Silence

Be relaxed. See that the muscles around the eyes and those around the mouth are relaxed. Relax! Relax! Relax! Relax!

Silence

3. The next three and a half minutes are over. We have had in all, six minutes of meditation. We move on to the third step. It is the step of serenity and peace. I imagine that I am like a rock in the midst of an ocean. Waves arise, distracting thoughts come to me, they dash against the rock. But the rock is unaffected, unmoved, calm, tranquil, peaceful, serene. So many waves come. Perhaps, I have done something during the day which I should not have done; let that not disturb me. I am a rock in the midst of an ocean, unaffected, unmoved, calm, tranquil, peaceful, serene. Perhaps, I have not done something which I should have done, let that not disturb me either. I am a rock in the midst of an ocean, unaffected, unmoved, calm, tranquil, peaceful, serene. Calm, tranquil, peaceful, serene.

Silence

4. We now come to the fourth step. It is the step of realising my Oneness with all that is. All human beings, all creatures, all birds and animals, fish and fowl, insects, even mosquitoes, all trees, and shrubs and plants. I am one with them all. I am in the lowliest of the low, in the poorest of the poor. I am in the meanest of the mean, in the most wretched, the most miserable. I am in

Him. He is not apart from me. Oneness, Oneness with all. Out of this cometh true love. If I am one with all, I am in the lizard of which I am afraid. I am in the cockroach which I want to kill. I am in all. I am in all. I am in all. How can I kill anyone? How can I criticise anyone? How can I judge anyone? How can I think ill of anyone? I am in all that is. What a wonderful feeling this is! No one is apart from me. Everyone, everything is a part of me, for I am the universal self – *tat twam asi*. That art Thou! Thou art not the physical body that Thou hast worn during this period of earth-incarnation. Thou art That. Thou art That. The Universal Self. Relax! Relax! Relax! Let your back bone be straight.

Silence

5. And now we come to the fifth step. If I am in all, if I have realised my oneness with all, I can never, never die. It is only when I feel I am this physical body that I live in fear of death. Now I can challenge death. Death! You cannot touch me; you can take away this physical body but I am in all. So long as there is one human being alive on earth, I am alive. So long as there is one creature that breathes the breath of life, I am alive. I can never, never die. I have never died. I am eternal, I am immortal, I am immutable, I am deathless. I am in every ray of sunshine, in every drop of rain, in every grain of sand. I am one with all that is.

Silence

By now your breathing has become deep. Be relaxed. See that your spine is straight. See that there is no tension in the muscles round your eyes and round your mouth. See that there is no tension in the muscles of your legs. Relax! Relax! Relax!

Silence

You are not the physical body. You are not the body-mind complex. You are the Universal Self. The One Self that is in all, in all that is.

Silence

6. And now we come to the final step, the sixth step, the step in which we breathe out love and goodwill and peace to all. "I love you all! I love you all!" Let that aspiration come out of the very depths of my heart. In the measure in which I give love to the others, love will flow back to me and I will always have plenty of love to give to everyone who meets me. Love all in the northern countries, in the southern countries, in the western countries, in the eastern countries. I love everyone. I love you! I love you! And I pray that you all may be happy, full of peace and bliss. I love those that love me and also who, for some reason or the other, are unable to love me. I love those that speak well of me and also those who, for some reason or the other, are unable to speak well of me. Actually call out someone by name, someone who you think does not love you, does not speak well of you, and say, "Mr. X, Y, Z, Mrs. X, Y, Z, Miss X, Y, Z, I love you! I love you! I love you! I love you all." May you all be happy and full of peace and bliss!

Silence

And now must come the final benediction. May all, all, all without exception be free from disease, free from ignorance, free from sorrow.

As you get up from this mediation, many of you will feel that you yourself are happy, full of peace and bliss.

Ask Yourself

- What is my stress quotient at present?

- Do I tend to worry often?

- Do I need to reduce my stress levels and alleviate worries?

- Do I want to be happier and healthier?

- Would I like to learn to live in the present, rather than worry about the past or future?

- Am I familiar with my deeper self, my true self?

- Do I want to switch-off from the noise of my mind and experience inner peace?

- Do I get upset or troubled by little things?

- Why am I not meditating yet?

THE SIXTH TECHNIQUE OF *SADHANA*: PRAYER

Let me begin with a story. It is the story of a worker, who attended the evening worship *(aarti)* at the temple, everyday. One evening he was detained at the factory, where he worked, and when the *aarati* time approached, he rushed to the temple so that he might not miss his daily appointment with the Lord. As he arrived at the temple, he found the *pujari* (priest) coming out of the gate.

"Is the *aarti* over?" he asked.

"Yes," answered the *pujari*. "It is over!"

"Ah!" exclaimed the labourer with deep sadness of the heart.

The *pujari* said to him, "Will you give me your exclamation in exchange for the merit of the evening worship?"

"Gladly," answered the labourer, for he had never wished to miss the evening worship.

That night, he had a dream. He saw the Lord, Sri Krishna, who said to him: "You struck a bad bargain, this evening. Your simple exclamation was more precious than all *aaratis* put together performed by the *pujari* all his life."

It is this kind of love and devotion that God needs from us. Worship, reading of the scriptures, blowing conch shells are all external rituals. But what God wants from us is devotion which comes from the heart. This is the devotion that is best expressed in intimate, personal communion with God, which, for want of a better word, we call prayer. In this sense, prayer is the most personal, most emotionally fulfilling technique of *sadhana* for every seeker. It is the most reassuring reminder to us that we are not alone in our quest: that God is with us, watching us and watching over us.

For this it is essential to have a pure heart. A pure heart when filled with love becomes a stream of tears. To keep the heart pure and filled with love, we need protection against the evils of the world. For this, we should invoke the blessings of God and pray that He keeps us safe and away from the alluring *maya* of the world. We need his loving protection; and we can attain to it through prayer.

At its simplest, prayer is turning to God. At its most mystic, prayer is stopping the current of your worldly life to give a few moments to God exclusively.

Let me explain: it is said that if a sailor from a huge oceanliner happens to fall overboard in the middle of the sea, and an alarm is raised instantaneously, it takes all of four hours for the ship to return to the spot where he fell in order to rescue him.

Sounds incredible, does it not? Yet it is the truth. It takes two hours to bring the ship's engines to a stop; and two more hours to retrace the distance it has covered when it stopped the engines.

We too are like this giant ship. We are so busy going full steam ahead with our worldly life, that it requires an effort to turn back from the world, put our worldly concerns aside and give God His due in prayer – praise, love, worship, faith, devotion, thanksgiving, supplication and surrender.

Prayer is reposing all your faith in God; not helplessly, in passive submission, but with active, dynamic faith that your life is safe in His hands.

Once, a holy man was sitting under the shade of a tree. He saw a line of ants, each carrying a grain of sugar. The holy man told his disciples, "See, how God takes care of ants. He will surely take care of you too. Do not worry, only remember Him." A young man, who was sitting by him and was desperately looking for a job with a higher salary, blurted out, "Swamiji, it is true that God takes care of ants. But their needs are limited. Man needs everything. Man is different from ants, you cannot compare the two." At that moment birds were flying in the sky. The holy man said, "Behold, God takes care of the birds flying in sky. Why will He not take care of you?" The man was not convinced and he argued, "Birds have wings. They can fly, they can go and pick up their grains. But man cannot do so." Around the same time, an elephant passed by. The holy man said, "Look at this elephant. God sees to it that he gets his food. O man, why will He not take care of you? He will surely take care of you, but you should have faith in Him."

A legend tells us that once God was asked, "The Creation of the Universe is complete. Now what is your next project?" God replied, "All my energies are now focused on my devotees, especially those who have reposed all their faith in me. They do not care about this world. According to them, God is there to take care of all their needs and wishes. So why should they worry? I am all the time busy taking care of them, because I do not wish them to suffer. For, they have put their faith in Me."

And yet, many of us lack the kind of faith that trusts God implicitly. We harbour doubts and anxieties. We do not really spend time in prayer. We have time for everything else, but we cannot spare time to sit at the lotus-feet of the Lord; to commune with him in silence; to say a simple prayer.

One of the reasons why we do not pray is because God has not become real to us. To many of us, God is a distant being. He is a far off, shadowy presence, dwelling on a distant star. I ask so many people, "Where dwelleth God?" With an uplifted finger, they point to the heavens above, as though God dwelt way beyond our reach. True, God dwells in the heavens above, but there is not a nook, not a corner on the earth, where he does not dwell.

I recall the words which are attributed to Jesus. These are not found in the Gospels, but in a less well-known eastern account of Jesus. We are told that Jesus said: "God does not dwell in the heavens above; for if so, birds will reach him sooner than man. God does not dwell in the depths of the ocean – if so, the fishes would be able to reach him sooner than man. God is within you. The kingdom of God is within you."

Alas, many of us do not feel His presence. He is not yet real to us.

Everyone knows the value of prayer; everyone knows it is good to pray; and yet, why do we not pray?

We know what it is to pray. We know the efficacy of prayer. We know how powerful prayer is. We know, in the words of the poet Tennyson, "More things are wrought by prayer than this world dreams of." And yet we do not pray.

Why don't we pray? That is the question. Why don't we pray? Whenever we are in trouble, whenever we are hard pressed, when we are surrounded by adverse circumstances, when we are passing through a dark night when not a single star doth shine, when we suffer from a disease that the doctors declare as incurable, when we face a financial crisis and are on the verge of bankruptcy, when we are involved in problems of personal relationships – what do we do? We call upon friends; we run to our relatives; we turn to our lawyers, doctors, to government and police officers – but we don't go to God. Ah, the question is, why don't we pray?

On my travels as a pilgrim, I have often put this question before people I meet. One of the reasons they give me is, "We live in a world of stress and strain. Ours is an excited, agitated age. We carry so many worries, so many anxieties, so many fears in our hearts. We do not even have the time to pause for breath – how do we find the time to pray?"

My friends, you find time for everything else. You attend to your business or profession. You make time for family and friends. You set aside time for parties, picnics and movies. How is it that you cannot set aside 15 minutes out of your busy schedule, to sit quietly and commune with God?

We need to know God. We need to move close to him. We need to make God real in our daily lives. And prayer is the one *sadhana* that can help us achieve this.

There are set prayers that some of us offer everyday. Millions of Christians all over the world offer the Lord's Prayer, given to them by Jesus: "Our Father which art in Heaven, hallowed be Thy Name…" Hindus repeat these lines again and again, *"Twameva mata cha pita twameva …* Thou art our Mother, Thou our Father art …"* So many of us repeat the prayer of the Sikh Guru: *"Tu mata pita ham balak tere …* You are our Mother and Father, we are your children."

We say the words, no doubt. But how many of us approach God as we would approach our father? How many of us turn to God, as we turn to our mother?

God is your Father and my Father. In times of despair and darkness, we can hear His voice – for He will unfailingly come to meet us. He will be there, when we need Him. All we have to do is trust Him absolutely and completely.

When I said we need to know God, I did not mean merely believing in the existence of God. You need to know God; you need to feel as close to Him as you do to your own father and mother, your brother and sister, your friends and your dear ones. Therefore we need to cultivate contact with God. This means not just going to a temple, or mosque or church everyday; not just reading long, unending passages from the scriptures, or visiting places of pilgrimage from time to time. You may be doing all these – and yet fail to cultivate contact with God.

So many of us spend a few minutes every morning muttering a few prayers. I know some shopkeepers and businessmen who never fail to utter their prayer – they are afraid that if they don't do this, they will lose all that they have. So we do offer a prayer every morning. Our lips keep on muttering certain words – but our hearts and minds are straying far. This is not cultivating contact with God. We say our prayers; we go to our shops, businesses and offices, we go to our schools or colleges, factories or farms – and we forget God. We must carry God with ourselves – we must take Him with us to our respective places of work.

Prayer is not at all a complicated matter. Prayer is something very, very simple. Prayer is like speaking to a friend. Suppose your friend were to come to you, it would be so natural for you to discuss with him your dreams and desires, your anxieties, your worries and your aspirations and achievements, your problems and perplexities and ask him to help you. Do likewise with God. He is the Friend of all friends. When all other friends fade away, He is the one friend who will remain. But how do you get in touch with Him? He is available to us twenty-four hours of the day and night, seven days a week, three hundred and sixty five days a year. He is ever ready to help us. How can we seek His help?

A poor farmer, returning home from the market after a long tiring day, found that the wheel of his cart was about to come loose. He was in the middle of the woods, and his cart was loaded with produce.

Anxiously, he searched his pockets for the little prayer book, which he always carried with him. To his dismay, he found that he had forgotten to bring it with him.

He closed his eyes and began to pray thus: "Dear God, I have done something very foolish. I have left my prayer book at home, and my memory is not what it used to be. I don't seem to remember a single prayer. So this is what I am going to do. I shall recite the alphabet - very very slowly - several times. Since you know all the prayers, please put the letters together and form the right prayer for me."

The Lord said: "This prayer is the best I have heard today - for it came from a heart that is simple, pure and sincere."

Prayer begins with talking to God. Later, a stage comes when we are silent and He speaks to us. Until we have listened to the voice of God, we have not proceeded far on the path of prayer.

In the beginning, we do not hear His voice; but let us be sure that He hears us. We may not see Him; but He sees us. And ultimately a stage comes in the life of every seeker when he sees God and hears His voice. For God can be seen; He can be touched and felt; His voice can be heard. He is more real than all things which we perceive with the senses. But to be able to see Him and hear Him, effort is needed. This effort is to awaken deep longing, yearning for God. So it was that Sri Ramakrishna said: "Yearn for God even as a miser yearns for gold, as a lover for his beloved, as a drowning person yearns for a breath of air!"

It is not necessary for us to offer set prayers. Prayer should flow spontaneously out of a love-filled heart. One look of the eye, one exclamation, may be more acceptable to the Lord than hundreds of set prayers offered in a mechanical way, day after day. Feeling is needed; emotion is needed. For, more important than the words, is the vibration of love which they carry.

God does not care for the form, the shape, the vocabulary of our prayer. It is the feeling that counts.

It was William Law who said: "God does not care for the arithmetic of our prayers, how many they are. He does not care for the rhetoric of our prayers, how eloquent they may be, nor the geometry of our prayers, how long they be, nor the music of our prayers how melodious they are, not the logic of our prayers; how argumentative they may be; nor the method of our prayers how orderly they be. But the sincerity and fervency of our prayers - how heartfelt they are."

You don't have to be learned or highly educated to be able to pray. Indeed, too much learning or education, far from being a help, becomes a hindrance in the way of prayer. Sri Ramakrishna was illiterate; he could not sign his name. Yet he prayed, for hours together. He prayed as one who stood in the presence of God, speaking to Him as a child would speak to its mother.

"Have you seen God?" he was asked.

"Yes," he answered. "More clearly than I see you!"

Truly has it been said, that God who made the world has no trouble being seen and heard by those who honestly want to know Him.

Art is not needed; music is not needed; scriptural lore is not needed; rituals are not needed; ceremonies are not needed. What is needed is a heart contrite and lowly, pure and holy – a loving heart eager to wait upon God.

Prayer is waiting upon God in love and longing. Without this, repetition of set prayers will not take us far. So often, prayers are read from books; they are good in as much as they draw our attention to God. But mere mechanical repetition is only the first step.

The prayers of most of us are entreaties before God, imploring upon Him to do something for us, to give us something of which we are in need.

God answers our prayer in four ways:

- The first is "yes." We ask for something; we pray to God, and he says, "Yes, my child. Here it is; I give you what you asked for."

- The second is "No." For a good reason, God tells us, "No my child, I will not grant your prayer."

- The third is "Wait." It is as if God tells us that the time is not ripe for us to receive what we want. So he tells us, "Wait. The time is not yet."

- The fourth is, "Here is something better." We have asked for one thing, but he grants us something else and says, "Here is something different, something better that I want to give you."

When the answer is in the affirmative, when God says "Yes", we feel very happy. We praise God, we thank Him; we call Him a loving God, a wonderful God, and our faith in Him becomes stronger.

But the other three answers – "No", "Wait" and "Here is something better" – it is these three that test our faith.

When God says No, the man of true faith believes that there is a meaning of mercy even in the negative answer. He says to himself, "If God does not want to give me this, it must be for my own good." It was Dean Inglow who said, "I have lived long enough to thank God for *not* having answered many of my prayers."

God loves us. He has a plan for each one of us; and His plans are perfect. If what we ask in prayer goes contrary to God's plan, that prayer is not granted – and of course, this is for our own good.

Our prayers are not necessarily answered in the ways in which we expect them to be answered. Not unoften, when we pray for flowers, God sends us seeds. He gives us the gift of toil and labour, so that we may grow our own flowers.

It is well to place our needs before God – but only in the elementary stage. As we grow in the spirit of prayer, as we learn to walk the path of *sadhana,* we will realise that our deepest need is not material things – "goods" which the earth gives and the earth takes away – but the Good of all "goods", God himself.

It was a wise man who said: "I asked for strength to do greater things but was given infirmity that I might do better things. I asked for richness that I might be happy. I was given poverty that I might be wise. I asked for prayer that I might have the praise of men. I was given weakness that I might feel the need of God. I have received nothing that I asked for. My prayers seem unanswered, but I am most blessed."

Man, it has been said, is the marvel of God's creation. His heart is said to beat 40 million times a year; his blood stream flows over a distance of more than sixty thousand miles in that time; his mechanism of eye and ear are wonderful; the qualities of his mind and reason are unique; but this is not the best thing about man. What makes man truly marvelous is that he may walk and talk with God.

People usually come to me and say to me, "Please teach us to pray."

I say to them, "If you want to pray, then start right now." The Divine spirit that is within you will lead you onward, will take you on the ladder of prayer, rung by rung, until you reach the very pinnacle of prayer.

Someone asked me, "Which is the best time for prayer? And the best place?"

My reply was, "The best time for prayer is now, and the best place is here!"

We must begin where we are. The following suggestions may be found helpful:

1. Spend some time in silence everyday. Relax body, mind and spirit by turning thoughts away from problems and fixing the mind on God. In God is the solution to every problem. When you fix your mind on God and forget your problems, the solutions will come to you spontaneously.

2. Talk to God as you would to a friend. Prayer is not just a formal, one-sided appeal to God. Prayer is conversing with God,

talking to Him as a near and dear friend. Talk to God simply and naturally, telling Him everything that is in your mind. Tell Him everything! Do not say, "He knows everything. Why should I repeat what He knows already?" Telling Him everything puts you in a receptive mood and you are able to receive what God wishes to give you.

You do not have to use formal words and phrases in your prayer. Talk to God in your own language. The language He likes is the language of the heart, the language of love.

3. There are many people who feel, we are so evil and wicked, how can we approach God? God is our Mother. If a child falls into a ditch and is covered with filth, what does he do? He runs to his mother and says, "Ma, I have become dirty, cleanse me!"

4. Talk to God, again and again. Talk to Him as often as you can. Talk to Him while you are in the bus, in the midst of your work, while you are at meals or out at a dinner party. Just close your eyes for a minute and shut out the world and have a word or two with God. Just lift up your eyes and breathe out an aspiration of love. This will make you feel that God is very close to you and that you are never alone.

5. When you ask for things in prayer, never forget that it is possible that many things you ask for may not be for your ultimate good. Ask - but tell God that if He does not give you what you ask, it must be for your good. Say to Him again and again: Lord, not my will, but Thy will be done!

6. When you think about your dear ones who are far from you, do not worry about them, but surrender them to the loving care of the Lord. You cannot reach them: God can!

7. Everyday, you must pray for those who have wronged you – mistreated, cheated, maligned or exploited you – or those whom you do not like. This will cleanse you of negative emotions like hatred, resentment, ill-will and anger, which are great obstacles in

the path of prayer.

8. Pray to God that you may be used to answer the prayers of others.

A poor girl prayed that she might receive a box of sweets on the sacred Deepavali day. The day arrived – but not the box of sweets. The girl mentioned her disappointment to one of her friends. A man who happened to pass by overheard the conversation. He had just purchased two boxes of sweets. Passing them on to the poor girl, he said, "God asked me to give these two boxes to you." The girl's eyes sparked as she said, "O Lord, Thou art! Thou art!"

An illiterate peasant once came up to his parish priest and said to him, "Father, teach me geography so that I can pray more effectively."

Astonished, the priest asked him, "But what does geography have to do with prayer?"

"Father, I want to pray for all those people who live in realms and nations unknown to me. It would be nice to know who they are and which part of the world they live in," was the peasant's reply.

It is only a few of us who are capable of such selfless prayer. As for the rest of us we are content with narrowing our hearts and restricting God's grace: "Bless me and my wife and my children!"

Let us pray again and again. Let us pray without ceasing. Prayer is the health of the soul, the strength of life. It had been truly said that if we do not pray for a day, we miss something. If we do not pray for a week, we become weak!

There was a woman saint who was found uttering those words again and again. "I like to… I would like to…" The people asked her, "What would you like to do? Would you like to found an *ashram*? Would you like to start a centre for social service?"

The saint replied, "I would like to climb the very peak of the highest mountain on earth and there I would wish to have crowds of men and women around me. I would ask God to give me a voice that would reach the very ends of the earth."

The people interrupted her, "Now we understand, you would like to deliver a sermon!"

"Yes," she said. "I would like to give a sermon, but that sermon is just of one word - Pray! Pray! Pray!"

Let this one word "Pray, Pray, Pray" – ring in your heart like a temple bell and awaken you to a life of fulfillment and freedom.

In the measure in which you pray, in that measure you are ennobled. In the measure in which you pray, in that measure are you strengthened. In the measure in which you pray, in that measure do you acquire the wisdom to face the trials and tribulations of life in the right spirit. In the measure in which you pray, in that measure are you impelled to go out and serve the poor and broken ones in the right way.

My friends, pray, pray! But remember that your prayer must be backed by your life, by your daily actions. If you pray in the morning, as you take up your position on the battlefield of life, and your actions do not bear witness to the prayer that you have offered, you are no better than a hypocrite. Therefore, let your actions bear witness. It is actions that God asks of us. It is life that he wants, not words. Therefore, let me close with the words of the great English poet: "He prayeth best who loveth best both bird and man and beast."

Ask Yourself

- Why do I harbor doubts and anxieties within my heart?

- What would it be like to have a friend who is available to me 24 hours of the day?

- Do I realise that prayer changes me from the inside, which soon gets reflected on the outside?

- What would it be like to connect with someone who can identify with my circumstances and understand me well?

- How can I feel closer to my creator?

- Whom do I turn to in times of trouble – my friends, my family, doctors, lawyers, bankers, or God?

- Do I feel disappointed when God does not answer my prayers in the affirmative?

- Do I realise that I can pray anytime, anywhere, anyway?

THE SEVENTH TECHNIQUE OF *SADHANA*: PHYSICAL DISCIPLINE

*S*hariram Brahma Mandiram – the human body is a Temple of the Lord, as the ancient sages tell us. I wonder how many of us ever stop to consider the marvel – nay, the miracle – of this bag of bones that we take for granted.

Can there ever be a more wonderful mechanism than the human body? Can there be a telegraphic mechanism which is anything like our nervous system? Can there be a radio as efficient as the human ear – or indeed, a camera as perfect as the human eye? Could we ever devise a ventilating system as wonderful as the nose-lungs-skin? Can any electrical switchboard ever compare with the spinal chord?

This is not all. The body is subject to all kinds of infections and abuse, in the unnatural conditions imposed on us in the modern world – a polluted environment, junk food, and the prevalent use of harmful substances like drugs, alcohol and tobacco – all of which impose terrible hazards on the human immune system. But God has gifted the body with its own defence mechanisms, which can right the wrongs done to the system, and restore its balance and harmony. Fractures and cuts are cured, as much by our own system, as by a doctor's treatment. The assaults of innumerable bacteria and viruses are fought by our lymphatic system. When a man loses one of his kidneys, the other takes over and keeps the system clean. Thus, as some doctors tell us, "It is not sickness, but good health, which is the greatest medical mystery!"

Our ancient philosophers describe the human body as a microcosm – or the universe in miniature. That which is not to be found in the body, is not to be found in the Universe. Hence the saying: that the universe within reflects the Universe without. Is not the body too, composed of the same five elements as the Cosmos – earth, water, space, fire and air?

The harmonious functioning of the human machine depends on the harmonious activity of all the components of the system – the body, the mind and the senses. When the body is abused for self-indulgence, we harm the system. When we exercise restraint and discipline, we put the system to the best possible use. After all, the human soul is a spark of the Universal Spirit, or God, as we prefer to call Him. When we live our daily life in the realisation of this truth, the body does indeed become a temple that is worthy to be inhabited by the Spirit.

Therefore, physical discipline, physical well-being, is essential to the seeker on the path.

Since the beginning of the Twentieth Century we have accepted what is known as psychosomatic unity of the human being. 'Psych' means mind or soul; 'soma' means body. Thus, the psychosomatic concept tells us that we are not just bodies – but an entirety that includes body, mind and spirit, functioning in a symbiotic relationship, in which a separation is impossible to make.

The World Health Organisation (WHO) defines health as 'a state of complete physical, mental and social well-being – and not merely the absence of disease and infirmity.' To this we must add, spiritual well-being – without which a feeling of 'wellness' is incomplete. I repeat, true health and well-being encompasses man's physical, mental, intellectual and spiritual states. When there is harmony and integrity between all these states, a man is in good health. This is the concept of holistic health that we need now.

Let me share with you the wisdom of my Beloved Master, Sadhu Vaswani, on the 'Science of Health'.

Sadhu Vaswani believed in the ancient saying: *Shariram Brahma Mandiram.* The human body is a temple of the Lord. It is the temple of the Spirit within; and therefore, it should be a Temple of harmony; for is not the spirit harmony?

Health is harmony, Sadhu Vaswani taught us. Very few people attain to such harmony, which is achieved when the outer body is in harmony with the inner spirit. The laws of the outer body have been studied with great care by Western physicians. Their medical science is highly advanced. But the West has had to turn to us in India, to learn more of the science of the spirit.

"The physical is not merely material," Sadhu Vaswani said. "In a profound sense, pure matter is pure nothing!"

Here are a few simple suggestions he gave to us:

1. Absorb good health vibrations from nature. For drugs, without the correct mental attitude can do very little.

Trees send out good health vibrations. It is wonderful to live in a house surrounded by palm trees. So too, the health-giving potential of gardens and parks cannot be over-estimated. They are the lungs of a city.

Sunrays are beneficial too. In India, we are lucky to enjoy glorious sunshine for most of the year. We do not need solariums or artificial sunlamps. We must allow the precious rays of the morning sun to kiss our bodies – and we will feel ourselves becoming healthy and vital.

Good health vibrations also come from the air and water, earth and sea. For Nature is a kind mother and a caring nurse. We must learn to trust her healing powers. Our doctors too, must learn to cooperate with Her in treating their patients.

2. Purify your *prana*. Modern medicine is beginning to recognise the importance of *prana* in healing. Hindu psychology speaks of *pranamaya kosh*: this must be purified. Hence the value of *pranayam*. It strengthens the nervous system.

3. Watch what you eat. Flesh foods, foods of violence may build up your fat – but they will not give you a radiant body, which is vibrant and vital. Animal food is unacceptable on three counts – humanitarian, aesthetic and hygienic. The trouble with modern day food and eating is that it is excessive.

Not all of us are prepared to live lives of austerity. But surely, every one must live a life of simplicity, if he wishes to be healthy, happy, strong and wise.

Salads, fruits and fresh vegetables are rich in vitamins. They build up health and vitality. Fasting once a fortnight flushes out the impurities in the system, renews and refreshes us physically and mentally. It speeds up the flow of currents of life-force within us. When fasting is accompanied by silence or *maun*, the mind becomes clearer and stronger. Inner and outer are in perfect tune.

4. Practise purity and prayer. In ancient India these two ideas were brought together in the one great idea of *brahmacharya*. Do not think that *brahmacharya* is limited to just celibacy. *Brahmacharya* can also be practised in married life. *Brahmacharya* is not asceticisin; nor is it stoicism. *Brahamcharya* is literally, moving with God. To move and to live in Brahman – that is to be a true *brahmachari*. He must be a man of purity and prayer. These two make the body and spirit vital. They rejuvenate the outer body, breaking the barriers of weakness. They link man with God: and he finds a great *shakti* (energy) flowing through him. He becomes a channel for the out pouring upon others of the spirit of Light.

Tamaso ma jyotir gamaya – "Lead us from darkness to light," prayed the *Rishi* of the *Upanishad*. The darkness is that of ignorance, ill-health and improper desires. The Light is the light of the All-Radiant One!

Our saints and seers tell us that the body is a boat that can help us cross the *sansar sagar*, the ocean of life. It was this boat that enabled great souls like Adi Shankara and Gautama Buddha to cross the mighty ocean of humanity and enter the blessed realms of God-realisation. Truly do the *Upanishads* tell us: "God cannot be attained by the weak and the unhealthy."

Here are a few disciplines we can practise for our physical well-being:

1. Fasting:

Fasting means abstaining from all food and leaving the stomach empty for a few hours or a few days. This is *not* to be confused with starving – for fasting is undertaken intentionally, with the aim of cleansing or detoxifying the system. By abstaining from all food and restricting our system to the intake of water or liquids alone, we enable our system to cleanse itself. During a fast, this is what happens to the system:

* All the toxic wastes accumulated in the body are thrown out – in the form of phlegm, faeces or gas
* The reserves – in some cases, the excess – of carbohydrates, fats and vitamins that have been built up in our system, are used up efficiently and effectively
* The body becomes light, agile and alert
* No harmful side-effects are produced

People today are so addicted to eating that they even snack between two main meals. Even when they work, they take a 'coffee break' or 'tea break'. When they go to the movies, they take popcorn or chocolate or icecream with them. When they have nothing to do, they eat just to pass the time. When they watch TV, they like to munch on something: Thus, constant eating has become part of our social behaviour. Some people even get up from sleep for a midnight snack.

How can the human digestive system function efficiently

when it is constantly misused in this way? It is little wonder that digestive disorders are common among the affluent nowadays.

Our ancestors knew the remedy for it: habitual fasting on certain days of the week or month. Thus, people in India still observe a fast on holy days like *Ekadashi, Chaturthi* or on certain days of the week like Mondays or Saturdays.

Fasting is an excellent process of self-discipline. It is one of the safest and quickest ways to rid the body of toxins. Fasting is also one of the best ways to clear the brain, enabling it to operate at peak efficiency. The Red Indians of America believed that fasting gave rise to wisdom.

Most religions of the world recommend fasting to the devout. Christians fast during Lent. Jews fast on the eve of all their feasts. Muslims fast during Ramzan.

Mahatma Gandhi fasted several times during his life – often up to twenty days or more. He fasted not only for health – but also for moral and political considerations. Even after India's independence, he fasted to reconcile Hindus and Muslims in Calcutta.

2. Good Food Practices:

Man cannot live without air, water and food. While air and water are available to us in the natural state, food is selected, prepared and eaten by our own choice.

The *Gita* tells us that food is of three types – *satvic, rajasic* and *tamasic*.

Satvic foods contribute to inner calm and peace of mind. They induce pious thoughts and feelings. They keep us in a state of emotional poise and equanimity.

Rajasic foods incite passion and give rise to restlessness.

Tamasic foods induce dullness, inertia and lethargy. They also give rise to impure thoughts.

Satvic food gives us just the right amount of energy – not too much or too little. But *satvic* food is easily digestible, leaving us with a sufficient energy balance to devote to our work. It is rich in proteins, carbohydrates, vitamins and fibres. *Satvic* food also calms our senses.

Rajasic foods give us plenty of energy – but we spend much of it in digesting and eliminating such food. As it contains energy-enhancers, there is greater likelihood of toxin build-up in the body, if this energy is not fully utilised. Ayurvedic physicians tell us that rich foods in this category generate stress, causing respirative, renal or cardiac disorders. *Rajasic* food also causes obesity, diabetes and ulcers.

Tamasic food gives very little energy – but is difficult to digest. It also generates a lot of toxins in the system.

The ideal diet is one that avoids *rajasic* and *tamasic* foods. You will not be surprised to know that what the ancient Hindu scriptures regarded as *satvic* food is now held to be the ideal food – although by other names! Experts call it high-fibre, natural, anti-oxidant, etc. and we are encouraged to eat more of such foods. As for what the sages called *rajasic*, *tamasic* food – the very same foods are now labelled high-fat, high-cholesterol, carcinogenic, etc. and we are warned to keep them out of our diets to the greatest extent possible.

Fruits have been described as the food of the Gods – and also the food of the *rishis* and *yogis*. They are nature's own special delicacies, brought to luscious goodness in the warmth of the sun. They are rich in vitamins and minerals, and also give us plenty of fibre. For example, oranges, grape-fruits and lemons are the best sources of vitamin C. They are also rich in a readily digestible form of sugar which gives us instant energy without the harmful effects of refined sugar.

Cooking destroys vital vitamins in fruits. The same is true of dried fruits, which retain their energy, but lose much of their nutritive value. Tinned fruits are best avoided – for they contain preservatives that are poisonous. For all these reasons, it is best to eat fresh, ripe fruits in season.

Vegetables are Mother Nature's marvellous products. Her Divine Garden truly presents a blaze of brilliant colours with the red and yellow, green and purple, pink, white, brown and mauve of these delicious wonders!

A vegetarian connoisseur will be proud to tell you that you can effortlessly put together a balanced diet just by choosing a bit of each colour!

Vegetables are not only a treat to the eye – they cater to all tastes and palates. Green leafy vegetables, tubors like potatoes, yam and beetroot, soft vegetables like zucchini and pumpkin, as well as popular treats like cabbage, cauliflowers, beans, aubergines, tomatoes, garlic, peas, onions – not to mention delicious herbs like coriander, basil, parsley, etc.

In practical terms food can be of two categories: food of violence or *himsa* – food that includes fish, flesh and fowl; the alternative is the food of *ahimsa* or non-violence – in other words, a vegetarian diet. During the last fifty years or more, medical experts and nutritionists have largely inclined to the opinion that a vegetarian diet is the best option for good health.

3. Eat less, not more:

Lukman was a physician and healer of antiquity. One day a man came to him and requested him, "Tell me, in a few words the secret of good health." Lukman's reply was indeed significant: "*Kam Khao, Gham Khao*," he said to the man!

Kam Khao means eat less. We must learn to eat less than we think we need. Quite often we eat when we are not hungry. Many people (quite unnecessarily) eat four meals a day. Still others are misled by false hunger – which is probably nothing more than sheer boredom, or lack of anything meaningful to do; so they resort to eating, only to feel forthwith, a sense of heaviness or flatulence.

We must learn to eat in moderation. Some people think they need to eat till their stomachs are full. But in reality, our stomach must be only half-filled with food; the other half should be air and water. If we fill our stomach with fast food, junk food, or an excess of carbohydrates and fats, we are bound to suffer from the ills of overeating.

I recommend to my friends that all cooked food should be eaten in moderation; and uncooked food like salads and fresh fruits should be eaten in plenty – I call this my "sun-cooked" food.

4. Exercise Adequately:

A lady doctor once asked me if I took vitamin supplements. I answered in the affirmative. "Do you take the real vitamins?" she persisted.

"Real vitamins?" I said, "I have heard of vitamins A, B, C, D, E and K. Which of them is the real vitamin?"

"None of them," she replied. "The real vitamins are the vitamins W – Water and Walking."

There are no two ways about it – physical activity of some kind is vital for good health. And physical activity must be regular, for its beneficial effects cannot be stored. Exercise must become a habitual part of our daily life.

'Exercise' sounds complicated. It may need special garments – shorts, track suits, leotards. It may need special equipment – treadmill, weights, exercise-bikes, etc. All this means spending money. And we all know – we do not always use all that we buy.

To everyone of you who is put off by the word 'exercise', my advice is, "Forget exercise. Just walk."

Walking does not need any expensive equipment. It can be done in any lose, comfortable clothes that you are used to wearing. Walking is easy and simple – and it can be done practically anywhere!

Lack of proper exercise, in addition to other physical ailments, also lead to stress, nervousness and irritability. Thousands of us swallow sedatives and tranquilisers that have harmful side-effects on our systems – when a brisk walk in the fresh air can work miracles on us.

Walking has been described as the queen of exercises. The reason why the *Sadhus* and *Fakirs* of ancient India were fit and healthy, was because they went from one end of the country to another, on foot.

We may be performing complex mental or intellectual tasks. But it is imperative that we should set apart some time at least for exercise – just as we always manage to find time to eat. For even the highest form of mental work can benefit from an increased level of physical activity.

Let me quote to you these beautiful lines from Thich Nhat Hanh, a Buddhist monk:

> The mind can go in a thousand directions.
>
> But on this beautiful path, I walk in peace.
>
> With each step, a gentle wind blows.
>
> With each step, a flower blooms.

Hanh tells us that walking meditation can be very enjoyable. This will enhance your awareness of the present moment and enable you to inhale not just the fresh air around you, but peace and happiness.

Everyone agrees that thoughts are difficult to control. While we walk on one path, our thoughts race on a million pathways. If we can turn our path into a path of meditation, we will find our benefits multiply!

It was Gautama Buddha who first initiated this beautiful art of walking meditation. When he came to dwell in the forest of

Uruvilla, he took his disciples on these meditative walks – thereby paving the way for us all to take steps to peace and joy.

5. Drink plenty of water:

It would not be out of place to say a few words here about water. In the absence of food, man can subsist on water alone for several days. This is because over 70% of the human body is composed of water. In fact, 70% of all the food we eat consists of water too.

Unfortunately we fail to drink enough water every day. Also, we fail to pay attention to the purification of the water we drink. Impure water, or water from contaminated sources can harm the system. The water you drink should therefore be boiled, filtered and stored in a clean container. We live in a world where people pay to get bottled drinking water – something that would have shocked our ancestors beyond belief!

Water helps to flush out the toxic wastes in our body. It controls the body temperature by being given out as perspiration. Experts have calculated that there is a daily loss of four and a half pints of water through our skin, lungs, kidneys and elimentary canal. Needless to say, this loss must be replenished.

It is good to drink water whenever you are thirsty. However it is better to drink water *after* an hour after your meal than with it.

It was a wise man who said: "Drink your food and eat your water."

No, he hadn't got his verbs mixed up. What he meant was that food should be chewed, masticated so well that it glides down like a liquid when we swallow it. And water should not be gulped down hastily – but sipped, savoured and taken in slowly.

6. Practise *Brahmacharya:*

A sage was sitting on the top of a mountain, silent, thoughtful, engrossed in deep meditation. His eyes were bright; his face was radiant. He seemed to glow with good health.

Placed before him was a jug of water.

A villager who saw the sage was so impressed by the vibrations that emanated from him, that he begged the wise man, "O sir, tell me the secret of your wisdom and the sparkle in your eyes!"

The sage replied, "I fast, I meditate, I sip this water when I am thirsty – and that is all I do."

"The secret must be in the water!" exclaimed the villager. "O wise man! Give me some of that water – and name your price!"

Reluctantly, the sage agreed to give the man a pitcher of water in return for a gold coin.

The villager eagerly gulped down the water and waited for a miracle. Obviously, no miracle was forth coming. Reviewing his transaction gloomily, he concluded, "I was a fool to pay you for this water. I could have gone to the stream and got it for nothing."

"Aha!" exclaimed the sage. "See, you are becoming wiser already!"

The secret of the sage's wisdom was not in the water – or indeed in the meditation or fasting; though people have always believed that these can lead to wisdom and emotional well-being.

It is of course true. But the underlying principle of fasting and meditation is self-discipline.

Self-discipline is perhaps, the most under-rated and least recognised virtue these days. I always say that self-discipline is the exercise of our *spiritual muscles*.

Any weight-lifter will tell you that he started off with light weights and then progressed to heavier tasks. So it is with self-discipline. We must begin with easy conquests, simple sacrifices and little acts of self-denial. This will pave the way for our spiritual progress on the path of *brahmacharya* – walking with God.

Unfortunately many people today are reluctant to deny themselves the least pleasure or gratification. The child must have its chocolate or ice-cream; the teenager must have his pizza and his loud music; the young adult must have his cigarette and his fast bike; and the grown-ups (who ought to know better) must have their drinks, their parties and their superficial social life. No one, but no one is prepared to give up anything. Instant gratification is the order of the day.

"Give up smoking? Impossible" exclaims a young man.

"Give up my whiskey? Impossible!" says the wealthy tycoon.

"Give up meat? Impossible!" exclaim several slaves of the palate.

Impossible? No! Difficult, perhaps, but definitely not impossible!

Sending a man to the moon was difficult for the Americans. Launching our own satellite into space was difficult for India – but we did it.

Self discipline requires effort – but its rewards are very many.

Alas, we live in a world where old-fashioned virtues like self-denial, self-discipline and self-restraint are no longer valued. Ours is the age of materialism and mass consumption. Everywhere, hoardings proclaim: Buy Now – Pay Later. Enjoy yourself – We'll take care of the rest! Borrow more money – no questions asked. Gratify, your appetite here and now.

They might as well tell us: Indulge yourself now – suffer later.

"Many are the keys to good health," Mahatma Gandhi tells us. "No doubt they are all essential; but the one thing needful, above all others, is *brahmacharya.*"

Brahmacharya is freedom from lust and carnality. In other words, it is freedom from the coils of the serpent, which is lust.

All the major religions of the world talk about the necessity of self-discipline, especially the control of the lower passions. However, Hindu scriptures have attached a profound significance to the concept of *brahmacharya*. As we saw earlier, Sadhu Vaswani defined *brahmacharya* in a beautiful way – walking with God. Literally, the term also means living and moving with Brahman – the absolute, Divine Self. In its highest form, it implies consciousness of the concept – *Aham Brahmasmi* – "I am Brahman." Thus, it relates to the effort to realise our Divine potential.

In a specific and restricted sense, *brahmacharya* implies the practise of celibacy and restraint of sex indulgences. Thus in ancient India, young disciples and students learning at the feet of a guru in an *ashrama*, were enjoined not to indulge in sensual pleasures and to observe strict celibacy, until they were old enough and mature enough to enter the next stage of life – the *grihastha ashrama* or married life.

Although celibacy and restraint are undoubtedly important aspects of *brahmacharya*, in a broader sense it implies conquest over passions – and the sublimation of the merely biological instinct leading to a profound perception of the self in relation to the Universe.

In its broadest sense, *brahmacharya* denotes purity of character, purity of thought, word and deed. It denotes mastery over the mind and senses, especially over the sexual force. For when the latter is brought under control, all other aspects of our life are automatically brought under control. Such a state of self-discipline is conducive to our health, happiness and spiritual progress. Indeed, *brahmacharya* is a virtue that will help us to lead an active and healthy life for a long period of time.

I am aware that people will find it strange that I talk about *brahmacharya*, which is associated especially with the practise of celibacy, in an age when sexual promiscuity has become rampant. I would only like to remind you that it was "free sex" of this sort that destroyed the ancient civilisations of Babylon, Greece and Rome.

Brahmacharya, as I have said, goes beyond the concept of celibacy, and it includes purification and awakening of consciousness. Such a state of consciousness surely cannot tolerate moral aberrations like the legalisation of abortion and immoral relationships outside marriage.

What we need under the circumstances, is a change of mind, a change of attitude, a transformation of the heart. Suppression or repression will harm us – while transformation of the mind will be a positive effort. And we would also do well to remember that an idle mind is the devil's workshop. An active, useful life with meditation and *naam-japa* in leisure hours will help us lead a well-balanced life.

The mind must be controlled and disciplined to promote mental well-being. Purity of mind is one of the greatest blessings a man or woman can achieve. Regularity, punctuality, clean habits, *sattvic* food and *yoga* exercises are all beneficial in the practice of *brahmacharya*.

Ask Yourself

- Do I want to feel better about myself?

- Am I willing to spend 20 minutes a day to increase my chances of living a naturally long and healthy life?

- Would I like to get rid of my body toxins?

- Do I want to lower my chances of falling ill?

- Do I wish to be in a state of emotional poise and equanimity?

- Do I want to protect the temple of my body and keep it pure?

THE EIGHTH TECHNIQUE OF *SADHANA*: MENTAL DISCIPLINE

Physical discipline and well-being are closely allied to mental discipline and emotional health: both are essential for *sadhana*.

It has been well-established through research and case studies that all major illnesses of the body are linked to negative emotions. In other words, a negatively inclined mind causes physical ailments in the body. Negative emotions create chaos and agitation in the mind, which affect the vital functions of the body. For example, anger and tension release harmful toxins into the bloodstream. On the other hand, goodness and sympathy promote the healthy flow of pure blood to the brain, stimulating the brain cells.

Deep thinking, meditation and virtuous living helps you overcome infirmities. They infuse vitality and energy into the body. Silence and prayer put an end to nervous tension. Tranquillity clears the complexion and lends lustre to your face. Happiness regulates your blood circulation. Sympathy strengthens the nerves, and generosity keeps your heart healthy and fit.

The Sanskrit word for health is *Swasthya* – which literally means 'to be oneself'. You cannot be yourself when you are ill! Health also means "whole". A healthy person is whole – his life is balanced and his energy moves in rhythm. A healthy person is happy, within and without.

Anger, fear, envy, jealousy, worry… in fact the seven deadly sins of medieval Christian theology – pride, covetousness, lust, anger, gluttony, envy and sloth – any of these can make you ill; more than one can keep you ill for a long time; and a group of them can actually kill you. A medical researcher, I read, describes the seven deadly sins as 'sins against common sense'! And these qualities cannot be conducive to the seeker who wishes to follow the path of *sadhana*.

We all recognise that other people make themselves unhappy, ill and stressed. "She is killing herself with overwork," we say. "He is driving himself into an early grave with all that drinking!" or "He eats so much that he is going to burst one of these days!" But alas, we cannot apply it to *ourselves*. We fail to see how we are making ourselves ill!

Every year, we spend millions of rupees on drugs, pills, painkillers and antibiotics. I am not including the soaring costs of hospitalisation or surgery – I am merely talking about out-patient prescriptions and medication. In fact, most people would agree that excessive use of barbiturates, tranquillisers and analgesics is one of the major social problems of today.

We could do away with all these drugs – *and* with dangerous addictions like tobacco and alcohol – if we change our attitude! In fact, a change of attitude is the first and most fundamental step in mental discipline.

How can we change our attitude? So let me offer you a few practical suggestions:

1. Take Care of Your Thoughts:

If there is one thing I urge my friends to practise constantly, it is this: take care of your thoughts.

Take care of your thoughts! For thoughts have power over you! Thoughts affect the body; thoughts have an almost instantaneous effect especially on the glands of the body. This is why we often say that when we think of a delicious dessert or a favourite dish, we begin to salivate – the salivary glands, in this case, are activated by mere thought.

I repeat, thoughts affect your body, therefore be conscious of your thoughts. Our minds today are full of wrong thoughts and negative thoughts. We allow our minds to be filled with thoughts of illness, pain, disease, thoughts of passion, pride, lust, greed, hatred and resentment, thoughts of ill-will, envy and jealousy. With such thoughts darkening our hearts and minds, how can we expect to be healthy and happy?

2. Stop worrying:

Negative thoughts throw toxins into the blood stream. Therefore, we need to constantly cleanse the mind of all negative thoughts, and replace them with positive ones.

The English word *worry* is said to be derived from an Anglo saxon root which means to strangle or to choke. How true it is, that worry chokes us – cuts off the air supply of hope and faith that are so essential for a happy, healthy, joyous life.

A worry survey was conducted in the US. It revealed some interesting statistics: 40% of the things people worry about never happen. 30% are in the past and can't be helped. 12% concern the affairs of others which are not really their business. 10% are about sickness – both real and imagined. Only 8% were really things worth worrying about.

However, I would say that even this 8% is not worth worrying about. It was a wise man who said: "Worrying about something does more danger than the thing itself, so give worry its rightful place – out of your life."

3. Give your mind a good shampoo everyday:

Give your mind a good shampoo everyday. Get down to the depths of your consciousness and cleanse your mind of all rotten, negative, unwholesome thoughts.

There is a doctor in India who says, "Keep your upstairs clean and your downstairs will be healthy!"

There are several psychiatrists who believe that many of us actually create illness in our own bodies. The body, they argue, is only a mirror of our thoughts and beliefs. As we think, so we become. Every cell, every tissue in the body responds to every single thought we think, every single word we speak. Thus, continuous negative thoughts or a constantly scowling face generate patterns of disease.

Body and mind are inseparable. The mind is known to influence the heart, the endocrine glands, the nervous system, the blood circulation and other vital organs. When the mind is affected by negative thinking, all these systems are also affected, leading to ill-health.

On the other hand, positive thoughts are healing, health-giving and vital forces. A happy mind is the greatest aid to a healthy body. By focusing on positive thoughts, we contribute to our own good health and well-being.

Mental alertness, self-confidence, freedom from anxiety and fear, and the ability to take things in stride – that is all it takes to turn your thoughts into positive, healing forces. This is why people who are mentally healthy lead better and happier lives than those who are merely physically fit. Equally, people who are mentally alert and active, continue to lead useful and satisfying lives even in old age, when their physical health begins to fail them.

Whatever we think, whatever we imagine, has a direct effect on our bodies. When, for example, you think, "I'm tired." your nerves and muscles register the message and convert it into noticeable weariness. If you get up from bed thinking, "I feel unwell," your body will receive the negative message and respond with noticeable illness.

Let me suggest a simple therapy to you: for the next 24 hours, starting now, you must resolve to think and speak positively, optimistically, hopefully about everything. No matter what your concerns relate to – your family, your work, your personal relationships, your health or your future – let your thoughts be positive.

This may seem easy at first, but you will soon realise how conditioned we have become to negative thinking. It will require a lot of effort to break out of this habit which is emotionally and spiritually crippling. We must consciously educate our mind to generate the positive energies which will lead us to good health and joyous living.

Positive thinking must become a regular habit with us. We must allow positive thoughts to diffuse down to the depths of our subconscious mind, so that they can begin to influence our pattern of thinking and our mindset. I have known healers who urge patients to direct positive thoughts on their disease-prone areas, so that pain may be relieved and positive energies flow into the affected parts.

4. Make the Right Choice:

As each new day dawns, we face a choice: we can choose to be happy, healthy, helpful and positive that day. Or we can choose to be dull, depressed, miserable, selfish and negative. The moment we awake, we begin to make choices.

At every step, in every round of life, we are given choices. There are always choices to be made – for God has given us the freedom to choose what we like, in the form of what has been called free will.

We can choose what we like. If we make the right choices, we will grow in health, happiness and vitality. If we make the wrong choices, we suffer from disease, loss of energy, loss of vitality, loss of creativity and loss of enthusiasm.

What will you choose?

If you make the right choice, the gift of a long, happy, healthy life is yours to enjoy.

Choose to accept God's love for you. He wants you to live life to the fullest – not merely exist. Accept His infinite love – and you will find that power and vitality and positive vibrations flow into you.

Begin the day with God. And a good way to begin the day is to affirm several times: I love You God! I love You God! I love You God!

It was an inspired poet who said, "We receive but what we give." When we offer our love to God, we receive His infinite love to us. When we offer ourselves and our life to Him, He makes our life blessed and beautiful!

Choose to spend a few healing moments with Mother nature. Nature is magical; it is mysterious and powerful; it is healing, inspiring and uplifting. The philosophy of pantheism worships Nature as Godly. The philosophy of transcendentalism believes that the spirit of God permeates all of nature. Our own *Isopanishad* tells us: *Ishavasyam Idam Sarvam* – All that is, is a vesture of the Lord.

Nature is a magical healer. When we spend time in the lap of nature, walking in the woods, listening to the music of the birds, tending to our garden or just looking at the evening sky, we feel revitalised, energised. When we breathe in the fresh air of open spaces and unpolluted surroundings, our flagging spirits revive.

Psychologists explain that when we are alone with nature, we let go of our social 'roles' and worldly responsibilities, and therefore, connect with the positive forces of the Universe. This is why many people unconsciously choose the seaside or a mountain resort or an unspoilt natural location as their favourite holiday destination. Nature can heal, inspire and transform. It can work miracles on our tired psyche and exhausted physical frame, and restore us to a sense of harmony and well-being.   4 - 1 5 - 1 7 ·

Choose the right company. Choose the right friends. We all know the old saying: Tell me who your friends are – and I shall tell you what kind of a person you are.

The 'right' people are not the ones who always agree with us. The 'right' people are not the ones who lead us into bad habits. They are not just people who are 'fun' to be with.

The 'right' people are free and frank people who are not afraid to pull you up when you go wrong. They are loyal courageous people who will stand by you even when things go wrong. They are people who give you moral support and instill self-confidence in you!

We can – and we must – make the right choices. God has given us the power and the wisdom to do so. We also have the choice to react positively or negatively to everything that happens to us.

The choice is ours.

Ask Yourself

- Am I aware that my thoughts create my destiny?

- Am I 'mindful' of my internal dialogue?

- Can worrying solve my problems?

- What is more exhausting – a day of worry or a day of hard work?

- Do I give myself a good mental shampoo every day?

- Do I realise that a positive attitude will make my life more exciting and enjoyable?

- Am I aware that a positive attitude is critical to success?

- Am I pleased with my choices in life?

THE NINTH TECHNIQUE OF *SADHANA*: SPIRITUAL DISCIPLINE

All that we have said up to now, all the techniques of *sadhana* that we have discussed thus far, are meant to achieve the ultimate function of *sadhana* – spiritual discipline.

Spiritual discipline can begin only with the realisation of the truth of the First Commandment of the Bhagavad Gita: I am not this body that I wear, I am the immortal *atman* within.

For so many of us, the identification with the body is so total and so absolute, that we are hardly aware of the spirit that is the indweller in this body.

One day, as I sat in my room, reading a book, a little bird alighted on my window. Opposite the window was a looking-glass. The bird saw its reflection in the mirror, and was startled. Little did it realise, that what it saw was its own image. It seemed to the bird that there was another bird in the room – perhaps a rival. Angry and startled, it flew at the mirror and pecked at its own reflection, its beak hitting the hard surface of the mirror. Actually, the bird was only hurting itself and soon, blood began to ooze from its beak. As the bird felt the pain, it grew angrier; it pecked at the mirror even more savagely, wounding itself quite badly. And watching this poor bird, I said to myself, " Is not the human condition similar to this?" Man perceives shadows and illusions and takes them for reality. We chase after shadows. We wound our own souls in the process. The material world, its allurements, the strong pull of the senses and the mind are far more real to us than this unseen, unfelt presence of the spirit.

Many of us are apt to imagine that we will attain happiness by the pursuit of worldly pleasures. Alas, this seldom comes to pass. Just think of the many millionaires and billionaires of this world; they possess everything that money can buy, everything that the world has to offer – pleasures to gratify the senses, wealth in abundance, fame and name, respect and adulation from every quarter – they have it all. Yet they are far from happy.

How true it is, that worldly fame and fortune, pleasures and achievements are but illusions! Let us not chase these shadow-shapes, for they will not lead us to the happiness we seek. The abiding joy that we seek so desperately, we will find only at the Feet of Him who is the Source of unending joy.

We return, yet again, to the ultimate question with which we began our discussion of *sadhana*: Who are you? What brings you to this earth plane? What is the true purpose of your life here? This world is not your abode. You belong to *Satyalok* – you are from the realm of Krishna. Having come to this earth, you lose yourself for the sake of a little pleasure and indulgence. You sell your soul in the worldly marketplace for a little sense gratification. Know thyself! Awake! Awake! Open the eyes of your soul and awaken from the slumber of illusion!

When man opens the eyes of his soul, he realises that he is but a traveller visiting this earth; that this world is not his home; his true home is the realm of Krishna. When this realisation dawns, he becomes a *jignasu* – he sets out in quest of God.

I remember a beautiful evening, when we set out for a walk with our Beloved Gurudev, Sadhu Vaswani. As we crossed the railway tracks, the Master's eyes alighted on a stranger who greeted him. The Master said to him, "Dear brother, tell me who you are."

"Master, I am a *jignasu* – a seeker," replied the stranger.

"And what are you in search of?" enquired the Master. " What is it that you seek in this Vanity Fair that we call the world?"

Beautiful was the *jignasu*'s reply. "I seek the world of Shyama, of Krishna. That is the one and only quest of my life."

When man becomes a seeker and treads the path of the spirit, he is distinguished by three vital marks – the hallmarks of the *jignasu*. The first is that the heart of such a blessed man is filled with a thirst, a yearning to attain the Lord. This is the thirst for Sri Krishna, the thirst for His Brindaban, for he knows that this world is but the play of *mayajaal* – the play of illusion. He realises that his true abode is on the other shore, where Shyam Sunder plays upon His Divine Flute. His heart yearns for the Divine Flute Player. He turns away from human company and seeks the solitude of retreat – a lonely spot on the quiet bank of a river, the shade of a tree, or just a quiet corner of his own house. Here he sits in silence. Tears well up in his eyes as he calls out, "Shyam, how can I live without you? How can I live if I may not behold your beautiful face?" He entreats the Lord, "*Tamaso ma jyotir gamaya* – Oh Lord, lead me away from the darkness of ignorance towards the Divine Light of Your Presence! Lead me to Thee, Oh Lord, lead me to Thee!"

The second mark of such a man is that he regards his physical body – the *sthul sharir* – as a mere instrument. One of the main causes of human misery is that man identifies himself with the body. Man has become the slave of his senses, a prisoner trapped in his own body. He wastes his precious life hankering after the senses, following their bidding.

Dear friends, this physical body is but a dwelling which we inhabit for a fleeting while. A time will come when we have to leave behind this physical form and move onward, forward.

The *jignasu*, the true seeker is always conscious of this truth.

He keeps his senses under his control, he maintains the purity of his physical form. He knows that life is a priceless gift that we have received through the grace of God. Therefore, it is fitting that we devote this life to the service of God.

There was a devotee of the Lord, an aristocrat who was often invited to attend the King's *darbar*. One day, at a special gathering held at the royal palace, he too was present with the wealthiest and wisest men in the kingdom. The King, in a mood of generous extravagance, presented each of his guests with a magnificent robe. The guests were delighted by his generosity and thanked their sovereign profusely.

As our man was leaving the *darbar* hall, he was seized by a fit of sneezing. His nose began to run, and he looked in vain for a handkerchief – alas, he was not carrying one that day. Instinctively, he wiped his running nose on the long, flowing sleeve of the garment that the king had just bestowed on him.

A few courtiers who saw this, rushed to the King. "Oh sire, this man has insulted your Highness, brought disgrace upon your dignity," they complained. "You bestowed an expensive robe on him – and he wipes his nose with it! This is gross abuse of your priceless gift! It is intolerable!"

The King was furious. He sent for the man and said to him harshly, "Take off the robe that I gave you and leave my court at once. You are exiled from my presence and you shall not set foot in my court ever again."

The man was deeply affected by the unexpected turn of events. In his anguish, he thought, "The King is a temporal ruler, who has bestowed a worldly gift on me. This garment is ephemeral, subject to wear and tear. Just because I wiped my nose on the robe, the King has banished me from his court. Ah, but what of the precious garment that the King of kings, the Emperor of emperors has bestowed on me?"

Indeed, the Lord has bestowed a precious robe on each and every one of us – rich or poor, saint or sinner, we have all received such a robe. That priceless robe is the human body. Alas, in what manner do we abuse this body. Let us learn to respect this precious gift, let us treat this body with the dignity it deserves. Every *jignasu*, every seeker, maintains the purity of this physical form. He guards his body from falling a prey to desires and passions. For physical discipline is an essential first step on the path of spiritual discipline.

If you wish to maintain the purity and sanctity of the temple that is your body, spend some time in meditation everyday. Without this practice, we cannot attain purity or sanctity of life. Therefore, as I said, the *jignasu* retires to a quiet corner, where he prays, "Oh Lord, keep me always in the blessed grace of Your Divine presence. Guard me, protect me from evil passions and desires, for he alone is safe, who seeks Your protection. All the rest drown in the deep waters of the *sansaar sagar* – this vast ocean of *maya* that we call life!"

The third special mark of the *jignasu* is that he surrenders himself at the lotus feet of the Lord. Let us all surrender, surrender, surrender unto the Lord! This is what Lord Krishna tells Arjuna in the *Bhagavad Gita*: *Sarva dharman parityajya mamekam saranam vraja* – "Oh Arjuna, renouncing all rites and writ duties, come unto Me for single refuge! Do not despair, for I shall release you from all bondage to sin and suffering!"

It sounds so simple, does it not? But let us realise, surrender is not just a matter of uttering these words or paying lip service to the Lord. The kind of surrender that Sri Krishna recommends to us can only be attained through absolute faith, unconditional devotion and unbounded love for the Lord. There are two *Vaishnava* interpretations of surrender which bring out this aspect: one version tells us: "Accept the doctrine of self-surrender and leave all the rest to the Lord. Your salvation is now His burden, not yours! Like the mother cat which effortlessly carries its kittens to safety in its jaws, you will be assured of reaching your chosen destination." The other interpretation tells us: "True, self-surrender assures you of Liberation, even like the safety and security of the baby monkey which clings to the mother as she does her acrobatic stunts across the jungle. But remember, you must cling to the Lotus Feet of the Lord for your life. If your hold loosens, you will have to blame yourself for losing the chance of Salvation."

Surrender in this context is not passive submission. It is an active, dynamic process of commitment to Divine Love. Such a wonderful state can only be reached through spiritual discipline.

The question is, is such a discipline accessible to all of us? My answer to this query is: "Most assuredly, yes."

As we know, the Lord tells us of three *margas* in the Gita: the path of knowledge or *gnana marga*, the path of action or *karma marga*, and finally, the path of devotion or *bhakti marga*, are all revealed to Arjuna by the Lord. He has been allowed to raise questions and clear his doubts. Repeatedly, he has asked the Lord: "Which path is the best?" Sri Krishna has assured him that all the paths can lead to the liberation of the soul. Yet again, Arjuna asks of the Lord: Who is a better *yogi* – the one who combines devotion with action, or the one who combines devotion with knowledge? For Sri Krishna had earlier said that the *yoga* of knowledge is difficult to accomplish – whereas the one who follows the path of action can realise the Supreme Reality successfully. Now, Arjuna wants to know which one of these would go hand in hand with the path of devotion.

Sri Krishna in his considered reply arranges the different disciplines both in the order of their intrinsic excellence, and also in the order of their ease of performance for the aspirant. What he emphasises is that though one of the paths may be intrinsically superior to the other, it is of no use if aspirants cannot practise them well. Thus, the focus shifts to the receptivity, the response, the ability of the students. The preference and the aptitude of the aspirant thus becomes the criterion for the path that is to be selected. Sri Krishna relates the various techniques to achieve self-realisation:

- On Me alone fix your mind; let your understanding dwell in Me

- If you are not able to fix your thoughts steadily on Me, try to reach Me through the practise of concentration and meditation

- If you are unable to do this, you can attain to Me even by performing actions for My sake

- If you are unable to do even this, then taking refuge in Me, renounce attachment with the fruits of all actions

Thus, we may see that the different paths to attain the Supreme Reality are placed in order:

1) Comprehension of the Supreme Reality through Rational Understanding

2) Concentration on the Supreme Reality through Meditation

3) Performing actions that are dedicated to God

4) Performing actions desirelessly and selflessly – without expectation of results

5) Single-minded devotion to God

The *gnana marga* is the most difficult and the *bhakti marg,* the way of surrender, is perhaps the simplest, easiest – and the one that is accessible to us all. Those of us who are at a higher stage of spiritual evolution, may proceed from knowledge to devotion. But for the rest of us, devotion must be the starting point to attain divine knowledge.

The marvellous thing about the Gita is that it tells us to choose the path that appeals to us, the one that suits us best. This is in tune with the liberalism, pragmatism and freedom from dogma that characterises *sanatana dharma* at its best. What matters is the spiritual discipline that enables one to reach the goal – not its technique or methodology. In fact, Sri Krishna assures us that none of us can go astray if we follow any one of the paths: *In whatever way people approach Me, on that way I meet them.*

In the final chapter of the Gita, the Lord integrates the paths to utter the final secret to Arjuna:

Fix thy mind on Me; be devoted to Me; sacrifice to Me; prostrate thyself before Me. So shalt thou come to Me. I pledge thee My truth; thou art dear to Me.

XVIII-65

And, even more emphatically:

Abandoning all rites and writ duties, come unto Me alone for refuge. Grieve not! I shall liberate thee from all sins.

XVIII-66

This is the final and most inspiring message of the Gita. It is also the quintessence of spiritual discipline. This is not escapism; this is not shifting our responsibility on to God; in fact the Lord has insisted that we should never shirk our duties – rather, we must free our mind from egoism and desire. Divine grace is obtained through unconditional surrender to the Lord. The Lord should be made the single goal of our life, the sole object of our worldly endeavours.

What are the qualities one must cultivate to tread the path of spiritual discipline through *gnana yoga?*

1) Viveka or discrimination. This helps us perceive the distinction between the real and the unreal, the good from the bad.

2) Vairagya or dispassion. You free yourself from slavery of sense pleasures. You rise above pleasure and pain. You remember the words of the Lord in the Gita: "The delights are born of sense contacts and verily wombs of pain."

3) *Shad sampat* or the six-fold virtues which are:

- *Kshama* – calmness of mind, achieved through the conquest of desires
- *Dama* – control of the senses
- *Uparati* – contentment of mind, that is born out of disgust for worldly enjoyments
- *Titiksha* – power of endurance
- *Shraddha* – intense faith in the scriptures and in the words of the Guru
- *Samadhara* – one-pointed concentration on the Lord – which is achieved by a combination of the above five qualities

4)   *Mumukshatwa* – or desire for liberation. The mind, heart and soul must be set unswervingly on the Lord. He must become the single goal, the sole focus of your life. The best way to develop this intense desire for liberation is to seek the company of saints and true devotees of the Lord.

Spiritual discipline can also be cultivated through *karma yoga* – the path of action:

- Plunge yourself into selfless work. Do your duty – and a little more. Work for the welfare of others. Selfish work retards spiritual growth; selfless work elevates you to lofty heights of true joy and peace.
- Selflessness grows but gradually. Work patiently and ceaselessly; bear in mind the splendid examples of the great *karma yogis*.
- Grow in the virtues of love and compassion. Put others before yourself.
- Dedicate your work to the Lord. Let your work become a form of worship.
- Develop the spirit of detachment, non-attachment to work and the results of work. Do not be swayed by success and failure,

praise and blame. Do not expect rewards – offer your work to the Lord in the spirit of *yagna* or sacrifice.

- One important function of selfless work is that it makes possible the purification of the mind.

- Be calm and unattached. Act with wisdom and understanding, so that you may acquire "skill in action".

- The motive with which you act is the most important aspect of *karma yoga*. *Karma yoga* is performed for the sake of God alone – with the sole aim of realising God. Name, fame, philanthropy, social reform, power, release from sin – all these, when desired as results, detract from *karma yoga*. If the motive is pure and selfless, it is *karma yoga*. If the motive is impure, it is not.

When it is properly understood and practised, *karma yoga* can give the aspirant rapid progress on the path of self-realisation.

Bhakti yoga is the path of utter devotion, supreme love for God. It is pure and selfless love, which is far above worldly love. It does not involve bargaining with God over results; it is above all selfish motives. It is intense devotion and attachment to the Lord. It has to be felt, experienced – not talked about or discussed.

Bhakti pervades the devotee's heart, mind and soul.

- In its intensity, all impurities of the mind are destroyed, reduced to ashes.

- It makes the devotee simple and childlike in his absolute trust in God.

- It has none of the weaknesses and defects of human love – like selfishness, insincerity, attachment and ego.

- It is the most pure and natural form of love – for we learn to love God even as He loves us.

What are the qualities of a true *bhakta*?

- He has a soft, loving, tender heart.
- He is free from pride, lust and anger, greed and egoism.
- In his great love for the Lord, he strives for perfection – and ceaselessly works to overcome his defects.
- He is free from all cares, fears and worries. Like a child, he feels himself safe and secure in the Lord's Divine protection.
- He treats everybody alike; he does not see people as 'enemies' or 'friends'; all people are his brothers and sisters. His love extends to all alike – for in each and every human being, he perceives the form of the Lord.
- His faith in the Lord is firm, unwavering and absolute. His strength and courage are derived from this faith. This faith roots out all anxiety and fear from his mind.
- He is firm in the conviction that all that happens to him, happens for the best – for it comes as the God's Will. Happiness and sorrow are also forms of God's Grace.
- his heart is a home of intense longing for the Lord. Out of its depths cometh one cry: "When? O Lord, when?" His eyes are filled with unbidden tears.

Bhakti too requires heroism. In its highest stages, the devotee even refrains from asking God to take away his pain, misery and suffering. Thus, it was that Kunti prayed to Sri Krishna: "O Lord, let me always have some littleadversity, so that my mind may be ever fixed at Thy Feet."

Surrendering oneself to the Lord implies giving oneself up to the Lord completely and wholly; and rejoicing in every incident, every accident of life as His blessing. This is true spiritual discipline.

Beginning with ordinary *bhakti*, which for most of us is worship of a form or an idol, eventually leads to *para bhakti* – the highest form of devotion in which the devotee feels completely one with the Lord. He sees the Lord in all – he sees everything, everyone as the Lord's manifestation.

Para bhakti eventually leads to *gnana* – the highest wisdom. Both *gnana* and *para bhakti* enable us to attain liberation, union with the Lord – which is the goal of all *sadhana* and *abhaysa*.

Dear brothers and sisters, let us therefore, stop chasing the shadow-shapes of worldly pleasure. Let each one of us make the effort to become a *jignasu* – a seeker. Let us kindle in our hearts the yearning to attain the Lord's Feet. Let us discipline our body and mind. Let us cultivate the spiritual discipline that enables us to surrender unto the Lord and seek *mukti* – Liberation from human life.

Ask Yourself

- Where is my true homeland?

- What happens to me when I leave the physical body?

- Do I want to be released from the bondage of sin and suffering?

- Am I a slave of my senses?

- Do I wish to cast all my burdens to the Lord and seek refuge at His lotus feet?

- In what way do I want to approach the Lord?

- Do I aspire to feel safe and secure in the Lord's divine protection?

Obstacles on the Path of *Sadhana* – and How We Can Overcome Them

The sacred *Upanishads* sum up the essence of a Hindu way of life in the following lines:

Let there be no neglect of Truth. Let there be no neglect of *dharma*.

Let there be no neglect of welfare. Let there be no neglect of prosperity.

Let there be no neglect of study and teaching.

Let there be no neglect of the duties to the Gods and the ancestors.

– Taittriya Upanishad

In the Hindu way of life, *yoga, dhyana* and *abhyasa* are almost used as synonyms of *sadhana* or spiritual practice. *Sadhana* is nothing but the spiritual discipline that is achieved by repeating the same activity (*kriya*) systematically.

Repeat and *systematic* are key words in this context. *Sadhana* is not a short-term course or a six month diploma, or a part-time occupation! It is only persistent and determined practice that can make our *sadhana* perfect.

The great Maharishi Patanjali himself warns us about the *antarayas* or obstacles which we encounter on the path of *yoga* – and these also apply to *sadhana*.

1. Illness: when you are in a disturbed frame of mind or physically unfit, you cannot undertake *sadhana* successfully. *Sadhana* is not for those who lack emotional balance and maturity. Negative states of mind like arrogance, anger, hostility and hatred are also not conducive to the path of *sadhana*.

2. Lethargy or *tamas* is a state induced by overeating, over-indulgence, or occasionally even by extreme weather conditions. We feel low and depleted; we feel 'heavy' in body and mind; we find that we cannot do anything useful or constructive. Our moods have a definite bearing on our minds, and it is better that we avoid such conditions when we attempt to undertake *sadhana*.

3. Doubt or *samasya* is a negative feeling which fills us with uncertainty and pessimism. This can also undermine our effort to take up *sadhana*.

4. Haste, leading to rashness and impatience is not suited for the *sadhak*. We will only slip instead of making progress on the path.

5. Fatigue or exhaustion, known as *alasya,* is also a debilitating condition. Our confidence is undermined, our energy levels are low. We need to be rejuvenated, remotivated before we can walk the path of *sadhana*.

6. Distraction or *avirati* disturbs our powers of concentration. It diverts our mind from the chosen path and may even lead us to needless temptations. When we are led in the wrong direction, we lose the power of concentration.

7. Arrogance and *pride* are serious hurdles on the path of *sadhana*. Those who are satisfied, complacent and vain, think that they know everything; they are actually in a state of *avidya* or ignorance and they cannot focus on *sadhana*, which is an exercise in humility and self-surrender.

8. There is also the sense of an *inability to proceed*. We are discouraged and disheartened by what we perceive as our failure

to progress. We may have even taken the first few steps, but feel that we are not getting anywhere. We despair of ever achieving our goal. This is hardly a helpful attitude.

9. Loss of confidence is the consequence of our own inability to proceed. We fall back and lose the motivation to pursue our goal.

These obstacles, as I have said, are mentioned by Patanjali. But they are not all. Living in a modern world of allurements and entanglements, we face many more such obstacles or "attitude problems".

1. "I have no time!" we proclaim loudly. We have time for TV, time to gossip, time to fool around, time to 'browse the web' mindlessly – but no time for ourselves, no time to discover the hidden treasures within us, no time to focus on the purpose and goal of our life.

2. "I don't live alone!" we protest. Friends, family, colleagues, neighbours, customers and business contacts are all entitled to their claims upon us. We respect their demands, but we ignore our own deeper needs.

3. "I have other needs!" we insist. We are anxious to make more money; we are eager to become more powerful; we seek fame and popularity, and we decide that *sadhana* and Liberation can be relegated to old age.

Aspirants who wish to tread the path of *sadhana* – whoever they are and wherever they may be – have this in common: they value inner peace, harmony and serenity. They are eager and determined to probe the depths of the true Self, and they have made a serious commitment to the way of *sadhana*. And in order to succeed on the chosen path, they make every effort to conquer both outer distractions and inner impediments.

In the Gita, we are given a memorable picture of a tortoise. Once the tortoise draws in its limbs, you will not be able to draw them out, even if you cut the creature into four pieces! This is the kind of determination you too, will need, if you wish to tread the way of *sadhana*. How can we cultivate such determination and persistence?

1. We must pray, again and again.

Pray with full consciousness. Pray to the Lord with utmost faith. Pray in the awareness that you are God's child and He will do only what is best for you.

Pray to Him honestly, in simplicity, with longing and sincerity. Words and images do not matter in prayer: feelings are far more important. Therefore, pray with deep feelings.

2. Seek the guidance of a Guru, a spiritual mentor. Spending time in the presence of an evolved soul is the most powerful source of strength and inner wisdom. A Guru inspires us by his living example. He sees the potential in us that we ourselves are not aware of. Above all he encourages us to believe that we are also capable of achieving what he has. He provides tremendous powers of incentive and inspiration. He cures us of crippling negative emotions.

3. Start with *Karma Yoga* – before you set out in search of the inner self. Even those of us who feel diffident to tread the way of *sadhana* can prepare ourselves effectively by undertaking acts of selfless service. When we go out of our way to help and serve others, without claiming credit, without any thought of reward, we automatically purify our *antahkarana* or inner instrument.

4. Cultivate self-discipline. The Gita teaches us that *tamas* is overcome by *rajas* – the principle of action, energy and dynamism. When we cultivate discipline of the mind and the senses, it will automatically lead us to *sattva* – light and harmony. With this enlightenment, our spiritual progress can be really speedy.

5. Eat right. *Sattvic* food, food of non-violence will provide us with the right energy and the right frame of mind to pursue the path of *abhyasa*.

6. Offer all that you are, all that you have, all that you do, to the Lord, in a spirit of *arpanam*.

This is the best antidote to conquering the ego and negating pride and arrogance. Whatever you do, offer it to God. Whatever you achieve, it is His grace, His doing. Therefore, say to Him: I am not the doer. I am but a broken instrument. If there are any shortcomings, any mistakes that I make, they are mine. But all glory belongs to Thee.

Stop saying *I did it. This is mine. I worked hard for it. I earned it.* Instead say: *Everything is Thine. The energy is Thine. Nothing belongs to me. I am Thine.*

7. Cultivate the virtue of patience. Remember, haste makes waste. There are no short cuts, no instant solutions, and no quick fixes on the path of *sadhana*.

8. Remember, practice makes perfect. Ask any great athlete, any great singer, any great actor – and they will tell you that hours of effort and hard work have gone into their achievements. The inner light we seek to find is one of the greatest goals a human being can aim for. Therefore, give it all you have got!

Most important of all, Hindu scriptures give us their own set of ethical guidelines, through *yamas* and *niyamas* (restrictions and observances). I would describe *yamas* and *niyamas* as an impregnable armour that protects the aspirant as he sets out on the path of *sadhana*.

What are *yamas* and *niyamas*? In simple terms, they constitute a code of conduct which enables us to live a successful life in moral and spiritual terms. We are indeed fortunate that the Hindu scriptures give us such an ethical guideline to right thinking and right living. These restrictions and observances – moral and ethical Dos and Don'ts – give us the essence of our duties to ourselves and others, which are fundamental to the practise of *sadhana* and a life of *dharma*. Maharishi Patanjali refers to them in two of his texts – *Yoga Darsana* and *Hatha Yoga Pradipika.*

In the context of *sadhana, yamas* and *niyamas* have an added significance. In the common man's life, they help him lead a life of righteousness. In the life of an aspirant, they serve as aids to purification of the *antahkarana,* making *sadhana* easy and simple. Several of the obstacles on the path of *abhyasa* can be easily surmounted by adopting these.

The *yamas* or restraints are perhaps the more difficult, for they require us to give up bad habits and negative traits that have become ingrained in us:

1. Practise *ahimsa* (non-injury). Do not harm others by thought, word or deed.

2. Practise *satya* (truth). Refrain from lying and breaking promises.

3. Practise *asteya* (non-stealing). Do not steal or covet what belongs to another.

4. Practise *brahmacharya.* Do not be promiscuous in thought, word or deed.

5. Exercise *kshama* (patience). Do not be intolerant and insensitive to others.

6. Practise *dhriti* (steadfastness). Overcome inertia, indecision and changeability.

7. Practise *daya* (compassion). Conquer cruelty and callousness towards all beings.

8. Practise *arjava* (honesty). Renounce all forms of deception and wrong doing.

9. Practise *mitahara* (moderation in appetite). Don't eat too much, don't consume food of violence.

10. Practise *saucha* (purity). Avoid impurity in mind, body and speech.

The ten practises recommended by the *niyamas* are the following:

1. *Hri* (remorse). Recognise your errors, confess and make amends. Apologise to those whom you have hurt. Accept correction.

2. *Santosha* (contentment). Nurture contentment, seeking happiness in what you are and what you love. Cultivate the attitude of gratitude.

3. *Dana* (giving). "Give, give, give!" was the *mantra* emphasised by my Beloved Master, Sadhu Vaswani. He said: "if I had a million tongues, with every one of them, I would still adhere the one word, 'Give, Give, Give'!" Give liberally and generously, without any thought of reward or recognition.

4. *Astikya* (faith). Cultivate firm, unshakable faith in God and your guru. Trust in the scriptures and in the wisdom of the saints.

5. *Ishvara-pujana* (Worship). Cultivate devotion through daily prayer and meditation.

6. *Siddhanta-Shravana* (spiritual listening). Be eager to listen to the scriptures. Study their teachings. Choose a guru and obey his teachings implicitly.

7. *Mati* (cognition). Develop spiritual will and firm intellect under the guidance of your guru. Strive constantly for knowledge of God.

8. *Vrata* (sacred vows). Embrace religious observances and never waive in fulfilling them. Honour your vows as spiritual contracts with God.

9. *Japa* (recitation). Choose your sacred *mantras*, and chant them daily. Recite the sacred sound, word or phrase given to you by your guru.

10. *Tapas* (austerity). Practise discipline in your daily life. Practise self-denial, so that you may light the spark of

transformation within you.

The *yamas* and *niyamas* have come down to us through the ages. They form the very foundation on which we should build our lives. They are fundamental to all living beings, who seek to attain life's highest aim – freedom from the cycle of birth-death-rebirth, and attainment of the higher consciousness. Observing them in letter and spirit will help you live the life beautiful, even as you progress steadily on the path of *sadhana*.

Ask Yourself

- Do I value inner peace and harmony?

- Am I eager to probe the depths of the spirit?

- What would it be like to have an invisible, invincible armour to protect me from the lures of the world?

- Am I willing to give all that I have got to seek the inner light?

- Am I prepared to commit myself to practise my *sadhana* persistently?

- How determined am I to tread the path of *sadhana*?